FROM MINEFIELD
TO MIND FIELD

FROM MINEFIELD TO MIND FIELD

LOVING AND BECOMING YOURSELF

ALBERT GLOBUS, M. D.

LIBRARY OF CONGRESS CONTROL NUMBER: 2014901847
ISBN: HARDCOVER   978-1-4931-6855-2
             SOFTCOVER   978-1-4931-6856-9
             EBOOK   978-1-4931-7010-4

All illustrations are done by Ruth Kathleen Globus

This book was printed in the United States of America.

Rev. date: 10/10/2014

To order additional copies of this book, contact:
Xlibris
1-888-795-4274
www.Xlibris.com
Orders@Xlibris.com
551386

CONTENTS

SECTION III—WHAT'S OUT THERE? FROM WITHOUT: THEIR ATTACK

Acknowledgement

This book itself is an expression of my deep gratitude for all who have supported me. It includes those that knew they were giving and those who did not. I tip my hat to those in the book itself. What I have written is just a faint shadow of what they were to me. They enriched my life and enhanced my consciousness.

There were others who helped in a more material way. First, there were my patients over forty years of working for them, learning from them, and enjoying them. Not mentioned in the chapter on therapists is Craig Johnson, PhD, who has been an abiding recent therapist and friend. The community of psychiatrists in Sacramento added to my understanding. Then there are the avid enlightened conversationalists and close friends, including John Wicks, PhD. and George Hargrave, PhD. Special thanks to my staunch supporter and helpmate, Karen Johnson, my secretary and practical idea person in my professional life for fourteen productive years. Thanks to Rosaland David for her steady hand and administrative assistance in the production of this book. Susan Fujimoto-Pierce and my wife, Elizabeth Globus, M. P. H., read and reread the manuscript. Elizabeth and I discussed every poem and essay. We are still married! My very own personal editor, Bob Middlemiss, told me the truth about my writing style and distinguished himself as a gentleman by bearing with me as I struggled to learn by his example.

My daughter, Ruth Kathleen Globus, provided the sketches for all the illustrations as well as the sculpture of the photos at the front and back of the book. The talented illustrators at Xlibris adapted them to the book's format.

Last but by no means least is the world of books and ideas which has nourished my body and mind and pleasured me night and day for most of my 83 years.

Thank you, all.

Al Globus

An Apology: A Poem a Day

So a poem
    A day
Keeps the tomb
    Away?

Writing a poem every leisure day
Keeps my tomb empty and far away.
Putting some wry, idle thoughts to rhyme
Keeps my lights on at the right place and time.

May any pain turn to pleasure; may any enjoyment last long.
I give you thoughts without much discomfort.
Friends, I beg you, be brave, plunge in, read on
Here, there, or even *ad seriatim*, in my poor effort.

I am thankful I write short poems,
Saving the trouble of making long tomes.

SECTION I

FROM WITHOUT AND WITHIN: THE CONFRONTATION

Prologue

This book is about becoming who you want to be. This book could be about you shaping your future. In my experience, most people do not change because they believe they can't or have become discouraged due to repeated failure in trying to change. I want to give you hope that you can change. So this book is about how bad I felt about myself as a young boy and how I changed. It is about how I worked throughout my life to be the kind of person I decided I wanted to be. I became that person.

Mostly I changed through my own efforts. Sometimes the change I wrought was molded by kind, skillful, helping professionals. Less often, the change I wrought was driven by life itself and world events.

You probably imagine that I have not always been successful becoming the person I decided to be. And you are right. But I have done well. At eighty-three, I am still working on and enjoying this task. It is not a hopeless task, but it does take a lifetime. Sometimes accomplishing this task is hard work; most of the time, I found it to be exciting and engaging.

This book is my way to help you to walk your own chosen path. I do not mean that you should do what I did or approach life the way I did. I do not mean to suggest I have all the answers. But I do want you to understand that you can fashion your life. This is indeed *your* life. Accidents of birth, of family, and of world events will impact you, but they don't have to stop you.

You are capable of sculpting your life in spite of and in response to everything outside yourself. The impact of things outside yourself is to make you decide to change or decide not to change. The inner life, which is the heart of this book, is the defensive tool you have already fashioned and will shape your life's course and your world. You are 100 percent responsible for your inner life. You have shaped the nature of that tool. This book is about how I chose my inner life and am choosing to use it in the future.

#　#　#

In the rest of the book, reflections follow the poems. My reflections on these poems or, more accurately, reminiscences of a painful childhood and of the experience of my first glimmers of hope will illuminate the relevant poem.

Reflections on "Love Always, Including Myself"

I spent most of my life falling and getting up. This in an attempt to achieve the first and most important step to being a mature person—that is, to love myself. As a child, I despised my freckles; my inability to read; my failure to be the focus of my schoolmates' attention, especially the girls' and most especially Dottie's; my aloneness; and my understanding of myself as being dull and less smart than my older brother. I saw these as deeply painful moral, physical, and spiritual deficits inflicted only on bad and selfish boys like me. During my adolescent and teenage years, my heart shuddered when anything happened to focus my awareness on these too obvious facts of my life. I knew it would have been better not to have been born.

I recall my first Scout campout—seven Scouts and four tents. I knew what would happen, and it happened. I was alone, trying to sleep with a back aching from carrying my homemade wooden backpack—really alone and as far as the end of the world from the others. I could nevertheless hear them whispering, tittering, and laughing. They were having fun. I could see the flitting blurred spots of flashlights beamed on tent walls and the wavering shadows of wrestling boys. I fell asleep hating myself as the one Scout who had to make his own backpack. I was cursed by the loneliness of a fatherless life and by a mother who only seemed interested in my future as a doctor and who, in public, defended uncritically anything I did. At the same time, she criticized me brutally and relentlessly at home. She generously administered random spankings bordering on beatings. Only occasional, whimsical, sparingly applied merriment interrupted my mother's modus operandi of criticism and denial.

In school, I could only guess at what the chicken-scratch symbols in books meant. Blinded by my inability to read, I blundered through the tests and failed to understand what the teacher said. Embarrassed by being held after school to read aloud while my first-grade teacher busied herself red-slashing homework papers, I squirmed and stumbled through a few words of the simplest primer. It was below my grade level. My mind focused on my stupidity and slowness. Occasionally, I was distracted by the certain knowledge and fear that I would be "helped" by my mother to learn to read that very night.

Floundering, I would read aloud *The Adventures of Tom Sawyer* to my mother under her threats. It was a book I could barely understand. She became angry and exhausted by my almost total inability to read and slowness to learn. Then, exasperated by my blundering, my mother would grab the book from my sweating hands and begin reading it out loud. She loved the book. I loved listening to it. I hated the experience and necessity to read it to her. I knew what this maternal instruction meant: a harsh insistence on sounding out every unknown word. Then a contemptuous frown reminding me that she had just told me what the word was a few lines back. She convinced me that I was dumb. I knew it was my fault. I lived imagining that these painful times would never pass.

But abruptly and inexplicably, my mind-set would change like a flash of sunlight through the leaves of windblown trees. While alone, I always knew I had a drive, a vitality that many others seemed to lack. My mother randomly and brutally punished me whenever she was too exhausted, too discomfited, or too alone without her adored husband, my handsome, dark-haired long-dead father. Even then these flashes of insight would show me the way to self-respect and self-admiration. I do not know if this insight was from God in his wisdom and kindness or if it was just the result of the hard-wiring of my brain, laid down after eons of evolution by multiple genetic accidents. Through the joy of diving toward the light blue of the black-striped pool from the high board, I knew I could—and I sensed that I would, someday—fly.

Even in my pain and constant confusion, I knew my mother loved me passionately. That love illuminated her life and gave her the energy to persist so that my brother and I could live "on the right side of the tracks." Her love for us and of her long-dead husband, my father, made her as special as I would be. That was her unspoken message to me. She knew—and I knew—the profound truth in what my father had said as my brother and I walked in our Sunday best to catch the trolley to go to church. Out of his sickroom window, he watched us fade into the distance, a pair-new-penny bright, young, clean, and with wet, plastered-down red hair. He said to Jo, my mother, "There go my bids on eternity." He did not add what he surely thought, "Leaving me to die, lying still against these pillows in this oxygen tent, dying from this damn disease."

I did not know, in so many words, that loving was my salvation, much less that I must move to loving myself first. By loving all of me, I would reap the positive, pleasurable response from loving others, not just family and friends but everyone. As I grew, it would become my guiding principle, often honored in the breach. I was bolstered by the knowledge that love of self must be wide-eyed, honest, and striven for always, even though achieving self-love fully is only a rarely occurring and difficult-to-achieve spiritual wet dream. For me, love of self remains the deepest of all life's panoply of pleasures.

Love Always, Including Myself

I have seen in both myself and others
The manifold thing that profoundly shudders
　　My hard-earned faith, lap streaked and weathered.
To those I know and knew, including myself,
Life itself has bequeathed love, a phantom elf.
　　Certainly, kind loving is by life inspired.

Bobbing up as passionate whimsy
Almost astonishingly, unerringly faulty
　　Yet love, the elf, yields all future's hopes.
Stripped of its promise of emotional aggrandizement,
Only the conscious purification single-mindedly meant,
　　In the very end, frivolity elopes.

To love without desire for self-return
Is an expanded eternity to earn.
　　This is to grasp firmly the meaning of life's meaning.
That, I propose, is the very essence of being alive in us,
An ascending goal ever moving from its animal onus.
　　This paradox: just as well, an inherent part of loving.
That the love within us expands,
Forcing us to use the invisible bands
　　That strap us to those dead, to be born, and living.
This surely is a divinely hard taskmaster,
This chosen path deliberately to master.
　　Spirit's key:

Whether due to Einstein's benign nature's being
Or due to a white-bearded God with robe flowing.
However platitudinous the ancient saw!
Enlightening love leading us is the law,
Even after our diffusing atomic dust
Has spread into an eternal cosmic space.

Loving Is Kissing My Soul

How grubby love can be:
Narcissistic, gratifying, grasping,
Aggrandizing, demanding, controlling.
Just so simple to see.

He says, "Go ahead, pleasure me."
She says, "How sexy I will be."
She wants a soft, heart-shaped rump
To entice him to thrust, bump, hump.

Had you not experienced its sweaty, salty pleasures?
Had you only naively seen it through a telescope
Or with unblinking eyes in cinemascope,
You would shun all of its rich and oily treasures.

But still my love does fly and soar
Like sweeping the arc of a pastel rainbow
Seizing the sun's yellow light in a prism and so
Flaking my deft heart's cry and roar.

The bright colors of strewn, shiny confetti,
Of lip, of note, of star, of bell, and of sun.
From Valentine's comic celebration fun,
A snowfall on my beribboned naked body

Had spun from my graying scant hair

All over my bare shoulders and on my knobby knee,
All over a miniature Rocky Mountain scree
Spread over rug by loving beyond care.

In passing speckled by loving, laughing Liz, my love,
Who enjoyed the mess of miniature arrays,
The signs of meaningful things loving portrays,
Two-minute red lips had anchored in each slipper's cove.

So spreading kisses, though the shining loving lips took a toll,
Are sequestered in warm and furry slipper's innermost location.
In enacting this, my silly pun, loving gift's informal presentation,
By my loving, am I not a lucky one to kiss my own soul?

Reflections on "Loving Is Kissing My Soul"

Does anyone you know ever laugh during lovemaking or, more specifically, during intercourse? I know of no formal study, but I doubt most people ever do. I never have. While getting close, establishing intimacy, during foreplay, yes—but during intercourse or even oral copulation, we don't even chortle. Although I have but a meager acquaintance with pornography, I do not recall any laughter, just grim determination to bring someone to the ultimate end: orgasm, simulated or otherwise. Sweating, heavy breathing, sweet nothings abound without even a smile. The predominant facial expression is an open-mouthed grimace. It seems as if the intense pleasure sucks the external communication of our acts inward, an implosion of neuronal nets derived from a coveted, almost entirely private, sensual awareness.

Sex requires energy. The pleasure of sex derives directly from the amount of energy available to awareness. It is astonishing that such an internal process melts our boundaries, leaving us to float in a space of unity with the "all" and with the "other" at the same time. Youth and fitness helped me, as I am sure it has you. Fortunately, such feelings and the accompanying scintillating and amorphous Zen-like thoughts are not the sole prerogative of the young. For me, this part of lovemaking has not changed with my senescence. Such feelings have blossomed with age. When sexual intercourse moves to lovemaking, what can compare?

Still, another question always puzzles me. Why are there so many songs and other works of art that seem to focus on arousing our desire for lovemaking? Since it is such a pleasure, why is so much effort devoted to driving the pleasure of loving home? Can it not sell itself? Without much conviction, I offer a couple of answers.

First, among the naive, who would ever guess that having sex was so intense, so desirable, and so all-encompassing? Think of this: sex comes first, then love. Sex is great from its beginnings in imagination and contemplation, to masturbation, to nonintercourse sexuality, to intercourse, and then to the border of lovemaking. Perhaps much of contemporary popular music is an attempt to sell sex without love.

Second, without song and mythic lore, could people really expose their naked bodies, thus making themselves so vulnerable? What about the trust required? We may need lying love songs to reassure us that something worthwhile really exists out there. Night and day and every minute, in every medium, artists laud this experience. Thus art coaxes us to be brave enough to move beyond our physical and emotional boundaries to open ourselves to the intimate penetration involved in sexuality.

Then confusion reigns. In my case, the discrepancy between this new experience and what years of propaganda had led me to expect stunned me. I was having sex, long overdue and long anticipated, but nothing much more than sex itself. I asked myself, is this really all there is? A good question without a good answer. This was something I craved and yearned for without reservation, yet the magnitude of the discrepancy between expectation and reality startled and befuddled me.

Life just kept plugging along. Sex had been good. Although we had never discussed it, my partner probably felt the same. I honestly do not know. Nevertheless, the sexual experience moving toward loving certainly did not light up either of our lives. The days pushed me along; with time, love came. Words for loving are not enough because the feelings and thoughts are amorphous and scattered beyond cognition. I will stop here as nothing I am able to write moves closer than light-years to the actual experience of lovemaking. I do not think that will change for me. I am just thankful that I persisted in searching for it.

Our Truth Lies in Our Eyes

Inspired by this line from the song "Rose of Tralee":

> "She was lovely and fair as the rose of the summer, yet it is not her beauty alone that won me. Oh---No! Twas the truth in her eyes, ever dawning."

It is said that the windows of the soul are the eyes.
Physicians claim they are the windows to our state of health.
Can one look into the soul and find the saving truth?
I, for one, would say only to disturbingly errant degrees.

Through all the senses, we have whirling worlds perceived,
Reflecting what we see as a bifurcated mirror.
Outward prospect is the universe, most beauteous—
Inward is a blurry world shadowed, by our memories deceived,

An ingenious, miraculous microcosm we seize.
A scintillating, although infinitely small, packet
Is given to us to know and thus to empower
Our purview of the vastness of all the knowable seas.

The galaxy of individual neuronal netting
Starred by perikaryon with receiving surfaces,
Infinitely plastic by design, or by accident,
Illuminates our passive thought and motivating feeling.

The truth lies in the eyes, and yet it is, I believe,

Crafted from experience, blurred by changeling memory,
Speeding past, stardust pulled like a meteor;
It is barely recognizable, a tattered and worn sleeve.

The doubled image, the outward and inward percent
Are but twins, the very same family yet different
Sharing and baring the stimulating genesis,
Cherished only during a life, truly a flashing percept.

How could we fathom what we could know?
The mind's image is only a vanishing instant of truth.
It is our frail grasp on what can be
A distant universe from the truth.
So we, fearful and hesitant, advance on what we can know.
It is, at last, the only comfort
And all that we really ever have.

Reflections on
"Our Truth Lies in Our Eyes"

The windows to our personal universe, our eyes, are transparent, emitting and admitting light. More accurately, they are like two mirrors in which the backings are opaque and are pasted together. This forms a truly miraculous interface. Backs pasted together form our individual concept, taking what is fact in the real world and making it into our personal notion of what the world is. This way, we know the world, but it is, in turn, just a hazy shadow of the "real" world. It is distorted by our personal experience. This, our individual reality or truth, is never quite right or accurate. It is always shaded, distorted, or emphasized, becoming inaccurate though still a reflection of who we are.

Our perception of reality is formed by our individual sensibility. For example, how we view ourselves as beautiful or ugly depends on our experience. Although we possess but a very small part of the possible perceptions of the world, what we do have empowers us. Our perceptions provide the playing field of our life's game. They encompass and structure the rules of our game. This is all that we can know, a time-locked but shifting concept moving from image to image as the seconds of our life tick away. This concept is made of two parts mingling like the yin and yang symbol—one gives birth to the other. They cannot be separated.

Thoughts generate feelings. Feelings generate thoughts. Our genetics constrain the scope of our thoughts and feelings. Within this constraint, our course is infinitely plastic and changeable based on whatever our will is. But once a course is initiated, the subsequent set of our future experience is forever a predetermined part of us. Time, the geological force of the mind's landscape, shapes it and eventually destroys it and us, leaving but our actions, a finite but tiny tracing on the evolutionary course of the cosmos—our gift to the cosmos. That is what lives on after we are buried by the inevitable, relentless march of time. The troubling yet fascinating part of this process is how one's inner and outer perceptions interact like backings that are opaque, pasted together to distort whatever the reality is. The more we comprehend this interaction, the more effective we are in enlarging and developing our collective humanity.

You Have a Long Way to Go

A comment by my therapist after one and a half years of treatment.

If I had ever stopped to think,
I should have known.
I asked for assurance.
He dropped me gently down a sink.

You never would have thought of his remark as love or help.
I certainly did not at the time.
It puckered like a taste of lime.
    After all, how distasteful the truth!
But showing a path free from drowning amongst sea and its kelp.

I had long struggled, staring darkly at a 220 plug,
Then glaring at air conditioner wires,
Musing on my helplessness, hopelessness,
    To have the courage, the will
    To be what I ought to be.
To empower me for life, to make me feel snug.

Perhaps my question had totally surprised him as well.
That I should be so helpless to believe
That moving from the deep pit of despair,
I had arrived. I asked, "Have I, in here, done well?"

From his prim, proper, but admired face,

"Yes, but it has been so slow.
You have a long way to go."
These few words escaped his habitual silence,
And a few kindly moments later, "Good-bye."

I longed for reassuring words that I had come so far
That I was already there,
Having come from nowhere,
That I had shot some nebulous, psychic par.

This man that had brought out my honesty, 'til then only desired,
To a higher level than just an idle thought,
To an inevitable, daily-living, essential choice:
A goal imperfectly achievable, certainly now pursued, subdued.
Perhaps it was more planned than it then seemed.
    He gave me a key
    To what should be
        for me:

To embark bravely, confidently, accepting help but with firm step;
To look down, open-eyed at the winding, venture-filled, branching,
mystical path;
To forgo trudging, a later lesson taught me;
To honor my power and my sex, also later brought to me;
To work, free of impatience, with self-forgiveness, yet later taught me.

They cast open the door to the vista of my life space, what I must do
    To be on a path unknown but of my own choice,
    To be an active part in its creation,
    To follow it, always, even to my very end.
In joy
In love
In creating
Charmed by joy's, love's, and creating's natural by-product: companionship.

Dedicated to Drs. David Geddes, Ike Kempler, and Larry Otterness.

Karen Said, "Larry's Dead"

To Nancy, a friend and Larry's wife.

You may think it rotten,
But you know he'll be forgotten.

We are a living whole.
Dying is a toll.
We know we should be remembered.
For lives through loving are tethered.
What lingers for a while are memories, the pain of not enough.

Feelings and thoughts are temporaries
Brought to life to weave a living fabric
That permits no enduring hole.
Pain of forgetting takes a toll.
From the warp and woof, we too slip, torn, frayed;
Living brings in a strand of new colored thread.

But the cloth is never quite the same.
With Larry gone, its color grows tame
Since Larry was a man who acted;
He changed our cloth forever.

We are the ones who suffer sweet pain of fading remembrance.
We are the ones who did not have him near enough.
To say good-bye now, so soon, is tough.

Thank you, Larry,
As long as I breathe and feel,
I will miss you.

Reflections on
"You Have a Long Way to Go" and
"Karen Said, 'Larry's Dead'"

I have been in therapy three times. Each time lasted about two years, a one-hour session at least once a week, with a time in between for consolidation and growth. This is something I always looked forward to. It is great to have therapists you can admire, even love. Never see one where you cannot say, "I really like this man." Not always perfect, they wanted to help. On reflection, as has surely occurred to you, I must have been really messed up to need so much help. My therapy was intense and based on each therapist's relationship to me. I loved them all. Now, more than ever, I remember them fondly, with their quirks and all. They were certainly different from one another. Almost randomly, each honed in on a different part of me—a part of my personality that had been left almost raw and only cooked through in spots.

The wisest thing I ever did was choose good therapists; I chose therapists I knew well and admired. I am not sure if my success in therapy was due to my wisdom or luck in choosing them. I remain grateful and astonished that my experience with therapy was so satisfying.

David Geddes looked a Mr. Milquetoast: tall, not heavily muscled, bespectacled, with thinning hair, holding his chin with his index finger pressed gently and quietly against his slightly flabby cheek. Steady as a rock, a pillar of responsibility and reliability, he had achieved some local fame in the medical community of Orange County, California, resulting from a long ethically driven professional war. He had worked for years to defrock a psychiatrist whom he considered to be a charlatan. David Geddes was a man of service at a time when psychiatrists were all thought to speak with Viennese accents, to be socially isolated, and to have a monomaniacal preoccupation with the idea that sex was behind all behavior. Another professional crusade of his was a long battle with the county bureaucracy, where I worked with him as my supervisor in the trenches. It ended when he got the powers that be to change the name of our *own special* Bedlam from "psychopathic unit" to "mental health unit." He was solid, placid, very bright, and contemplative. He was always there, always on time, always thoughtful, and ever a staunch believer in his patient's capability to work through anything. He applied steady yet patient pressure to help me grow toward everything I ought to be and could be. Little things expressed this belief, such as when he asked me to pick up a camera for him in Germany. It was something my dad might have asked of me had he lived. It showed David's confidence in me, bringing a euphoric rush of self-worth. Odd, is it not, what power seemingly minor things have to change people. Did anyone whom you admired put trust in you, making you realize that they knew you were completely worthy of that trust?

David Geddes brought me gently to deeper understanding through a dream. In my dream, I was waiting in a doctor's office. Many patients crowded the room. All who waited there had a bizarre, ill-tuned, and broken musical instrument with them. I was afraid. When I entered the examining room, the doctor immediately told me that my future was hopeless as I had a damaged instrument. My despair awoke me. Shortly before having this dream, I had had a vasectomy and knew, at some less than conscious level, that I would soon be divorced and then remarry and be childless. That would be a sorrow for me. David helped me to be a father to my children even after I was divorced, and he guided me to the realization that it was not a shame to love another woman, even though my then current wife was a fine person.

However, his greatest gift to me was that he helped me to feel troubled by the half-truths I communicated to myself and to others whom I loved. Then, such small and big lies were my daily, dissatisfying spiritual diet. This uneasiness made change possible, even inevitable. I left therapy still needing to do much, but accepting how I would feel—sometimes good and sometimes bad—while being honest and open with myself and with those I loved.

I would like to tell you about Ike Kempler. He was a lithe small man. His corner office, high up in a high-rise, overlooked Balboa Island, Newport Beach, and the blue reach of the Pacific Ocean. I now know something of his personal life. Many years after I terminated therapy with him, he and his family attended a seminar in which I was a speaker. My therapy with him ended several years after I had last seen him in session, when he wrote a kindly but firm note asking me to pay up on the small remaining bill. By paying this bill, I left Ike's world reluctantly and with sadness. Having that small unpaid balance was a link, somewhat like my scant, tattered, fading, and hopeless tie to my dead father. I was in my thirties. Leaving a comforting world of understanding and mutual affection is a road that dwindles to a path and then into wilderness forging one's own way. That is a tough business.

Although my father had died when I was six, I could never remember feeling the pain of missing him. After all, he was a prisoner of an oxygen tent. His shortness of breath isolated him by the fear that I and my brother would catch his pulmonary disease. The impact of his death was multiplied by my failure to grieve. There was a session with Ike Kempler in which I cried like a four-year-old-boy on recalling my father's gentle but firm discipline of me from his sickbed for my going out in the cold without a sweater. On leaving Ike's office, I immediately canceled my workday and made a silent pilgrimage to the house on Thirty-Fourth Street in San Bernadino, where my father died in 1938. I gazed in silence, absent of thought for how long I do not know, at the Christmas tree in the front of the house that we had planted the year he died. It towered above the small home we had occupied at the time of his death. Death came from a horrible, lingering disease—tuberculosis. I knocked on the door, told the surprised housewife the story of her Christmas tree's planting, and gave her my name and address. I asked her to call me if they ever wanted to cut the tree down. I would have dug it up then and there to truck it to my home for transplanting. I can still smell the pine.

Ike heard my dreams. The first was *really* a nightmare. I was making a house call, something I routinely did when I was a family doctor. I had come to see a tired, unhappy, irascible, and demanding woman who, of course, looked like my mother. If you choose the adventure of looking deeply into your life, you will see many "Moms" and "Dads." In the dream, I sat down next to this old woman on a small love seat with a rococo paisley pattern. I told her about my desire to buy a sports car. When I was a freshman in high school, my mother had thwarted my teenage savage lust for a racy-yellow Cord convertible. *You remember the Cord:* a rare vintage *racing* automobile. She refused to sign the papers even though I had already earned and saved the full purchase price through my own efforts and even though I fervently promised not to drive it until I was of age. Returning to the dream, when I tried to take the old lady's blood pressure on her left arm, she quickly reached out for my crotch with her right hand and grabbed my balls! She looked angry and threatening. I awoke immediately before the inevitable happened.

In a companion dream that looked to a future path for me, I was flying a biplane. Flying has always been a special thing for me. The plane moved from one aerobatic maneuver to another, but not smoothly. I was seated in front of and between the legs of a woman who had her hands over my hands on the stick used to control the plane. I'm sure you get the sexual implication. Insight came with the awareness of my grief over the loss of my father combined with the understanding of my voluntary readiness to let the women in my life take control. This awareness made it possible, though not easy, for me to make my own decisions. Oddly, the women in my life had little, if any, real interest in dominating our decision making. I realized I wanted, needed, and sometimes even demanded that women decide things for me. What a break that was. Shortly after the enlightening interpretation of these dreams, I came to live or die by my own decisions about everything I did or did not do. It didn't matter if what I was doing was in my direct self-interest or if it was with or for others.

Larry Otterness was number three. His most obvious and defining feature was his wit, which he expressed directly and with arresting honesty. Being excruciatingly comical made his honesty palatable. There is a French proverb that goes something like this: "You cannot open your mouth to laugh without opening your mind." Or perhaps there is no such proverb. But if not, there ought to be. Matter-of-fact, tall, and so ugly in a strongly masculine way as to be paradoxically handsome, Larry modeled self-love for me. He loved all of himself. He laughed in a most serious way at his panoply of talents and deficiencies. I often reflected that there are some things too serious to not laugh about them. Besides helping me to learn from and bear up under a financial catastrophe, he was instrumental in giving me the courage to give up my professorship. Perhaps you have had a fork in the road like this. This position was a safe job, offering nondemanding work and all kinds of benefits. But it also required an exceedingly great capacity for my tolerating boredom and hypocrisy as well as wasting *my* precious and dwindling time. Larry didn't believe in dream interpretation, but I told him about a dream in which I was at my writing desk at home. Dust covered my books, papers, and desk. I sat quietly in a rocking chair. Dust and cobwebs covered me. Suddenly, I sneezed. A great cloud of dust enveloped the chair, the desk, and me. It gradually cleared, but I had totally vanished. Nothing was left but my books and papers. The only evidence that I had been there was the dustless imprint of my body on the chair. Larry helped me relinquish a sure thing for the expanding, often trying, life I now lead. After all, what is wrong for you is wrong, despite your hopes to the contrary. And this realization must be accepted however costly that acceptance. To act on this more often than not garners ridicule or loss of creature comforts. All this engenders fear. So what? You may ask. It is more fun to be your own person, though admittedly harder, sticking to your own way, with or without being accepted or valued.

The essential essence of therapy is to fix what is wrong with you, whether it be the most common condition, your fault, or the fault of happenstance, such as parenting or societal circumstances. Here is my recipe for therapy: find someone you can trust. Someone who can listen to you. Not necessarily someone who is perfect, but someone with whom it is not difficult to form your safe version of intimacy. Stay with this person until your working together has finished that chapter of your book. Just as the God within and outside of you would, you can then pronounce it "good." Rest awhile. During your growth spurt, you will inevitably come upon still other things that need fixing. Repeat as necessary. The break with early life experiences and their results (habits of living) leave you in charge but also leave you with exposed and painful raw defects. You must learn a new life, and while chancy, it is fun and exciting. It is awareness through intimacy that can alleviate the pain of your defects and empower moving on to be what you want to be. It may be hard work. It may be a struggle. It may be surprisingly easy and enthralling. Why not? Is anything else more worthwhile? I think not.

Mismatched Socks Wear Well

"Hey, don't you know
That your great toe
On the right is covered by a sock of gray?
And the left toe is covered by black, I say!"

Looking down, somewhat surprised—
Embarrassed, my face I comprised
To hide an overwhelming feeling of disorder.
One foot was differently shod than the other.

It was just another trivial instance
Of life tilting my mental stance.
It was just another of those days
That leaves me in a scattered daze.

I sallied forth fresh from shower and shave,
At the height of fashion intending to behave,
To correct financial chaos from bills I neglected
And to work to pay some bills I had selected.

Now understand, this unsolicited, jovial, joshing remark
Had pierced my fragile intrapsychic bull's-eye mark.
Smashed to splintered shards, my equanimity
Reminded me of my present vulnerability.

Moving to a mode of damage repair,

I commented with careful, carefree air,
"Ah, no, no, they are certainly not mismatched at all.
I have a pair just like them in my drawer in the hall."

On guard, I thought, *The difference between*
You and me is that such a pair I have seen
At home in my darkest drawer, while you walk with matched pair,
Not being able to laugh at your hidden, fumbling, human despair.
You are not aware of your colorless bumbling,
My clothes, though mismatched, I am enjoying.

You can take it from there!
All know that life's unfair.
I can only do my best.
When I fail the test,
Some may cuttingly rave and rant.
Then I consider, "That is simply cant!"

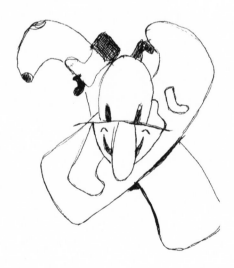

Reflections on "Mismatched Socks Wear Well"

Life is demanding. It requires energy and resources. For me, these are definitely in short supply. Many events afflict my consciousness. Often they are threats of impending doom or simply an overwhelming multiplicity of annoying inconveniences. How I see my inevitable mistakes shapes how I feel. I am sure I am not alone in this.

An example is an episode from when I was in my third year of medical school. I attended Northwestern University Medical School. I lived on the south side of Chicago. It was an unsavory locality. My wife, my two children, and I enjoyed public housing. I struggled to afford a two-bedroom apartment designed for the indigent.

Across the street from our concrete and cinder-block high-rise was the Green Gables Hotel, which I suspected let its rooms by the hour with a surcharge for the finicky who wanted clean sheets. Two blocks away was Twenty-Ninth Street, a mishmash of gloomy and dirty bars, which sported blues bands and singers, and a few struggling businesses, as well as some restaurants and pool halls. One takeout restaurant sold Cajun shrimp, which went well with Pepsi at three in the morning. I would often take it out on my way back from my job. My job was to be on call to crossmatch blood six nights a week for a Catholic hospital specializing in obstetrics and gynecology. I was frequently called to the hospital when a woman was miscarrying, as every case had to have two units of blood ready to go in case of a serious uterine hemorrhage. When traveling to and from the hospital, I always donned a white coat and, stuffed in its pocket, an old stethoscope that my dad had used forty years earlier. I had no need for a stethoscope at the laboratory. I thought of it as a talisman to protect me from muggers, as they would mistake me for a physician working in an emergency room. I hoped they feared being shot by an irate victim some night, and if so, they would want to have ER doctors healthy and available. Whether it worked that way or not, I do not know, but no one ever bothered me.

Chicago is known as the Windy City. It should have been known as the Windy Icy City. One night was so cold and the chill factor from the wind so great that snot froze in my nostrils. The telephone rang at 2:30 a.m. just after the bars had closed. I was jarred from a deep sleep made necessary by my pressured and frenetic life as a third-year medical student who was married, had two young children, and was on call seventy-two hours per week. Groggily, I answered the phone, expecting the hospital's operator calling for a crossmatch or two.

It was much worse than that. The voice on the line was that of my mother. This was a dreaded call; it had me sitting up in a flash. No, it was not an emergency, just a surprise visit. I thought of the intoxicated and exhausted barflies dumped into the fearsome icy streets. Wasn't that just too nice? She had flown in, not bothering to tell me or my wife of her intentions. She was at O'Hara Airport, forty miles away. We were not rich. Even if we had been, my mother would never have considered a hotel till morning, nor would I have had the courage to suggest it. I was not troubled about being awoken, about being exhausted, about driving out on a foul night, or about the fact that my wife, long-suffering, feared and detested my mother's sarcasm and sense of entitlement. Rather, I feared my mother's stay. How long would she stay? How many arguments would we have? How much damage control would I have to mount to protect my family? How much emotional rehabilitation would be necessary for my wife after she left? My wife was not accustomed to remarks that were born of Mother's disappointment, sadness, and anger. I was, by now, inured to her bitter and sarcastic remarks, but they had inflicted war wounds that had never healed. They were not bad enough to kill me, but they were bad enough to deform my character and my relationships and, therefore, my life.

Her visit and the night made these wounds raw and newly tender. Suddenly it dawned on me that she might stay for weeks! I knew my childhood wounds would never heal. They would not until I forced them from my life by years of therapy, much exercise of will, and the passage of a decade. Had I not been an atheist, I would have prayed for a short and not too uncomfortable visit. I comforted myself by reminding myself that I had driven out in the middle of a foul night—that might soften her. Then I thought how tired she must be after the long flight from California. Being tired made my mother dangerous.

That she loved me and that she would try to work herself into an early grave for me, I never doubted. I was as certain of this as I was acutely aware that she could not enjoy my success, that she would never let a single compliment slip from her lips when I was present, that she would undermine my efforts at autonomy, and that she would everlastingly remind me of her substantial sacrifices on my behalf. This seemed de rigueur for a tough Irish mother who had brought up my brother and me alone "by the hair of our heads," as she was so fond of telling us when in a rage.

The milk of my mother's life was soured by the untimely death of my charming and accomplished father. Therapists say that marriages are made to compliment the strengths and mitigate the weaknesses of the husband and wife. People's characters in a successful marriage fit like a key in a lock. While my father was charming, polite, fun loving, and socially adept, my mother was harsh, a workaholic not capable of play, given to slashing commentary, and possessed of an abundantly hostile sense of humor. Her humor made me both laugh and cry simultaneously. Earlier in my life, I had forgotten the humor, but remembered every detail of what made me cry. But this was not the worst of her awesome presence. She hemorrhaged feelings every day after my father breathed his last blood-filled breath. She was pale with chronic depression spiced with irritability. It was excruciating to witness and share her unremitting agony with my brother and me. That love-born agony she refused to mitigate with a new, but certain to be lesser, husband than my deceased father was. My brother and I had her all to ourselves, all the time, every minute of our youth. I dreaded her sudden and unannounced visit but hoped against experience that it would go well for us all. A smooth pickup and some blarney would help.

As the elevator did not work, I struggled down thirteen floors of echoing and cold stairs while I planned the drive to the airport. The Chevy that my wife brought to our marriage was far more reliable than I. I never doubted it would start. I headed out. The night was as black and starless as my mood, the wind as piercing as my mother's anticipated critique of my life, my family, and my work, and the streets as slippery and as dangerous from ice as the forthcoming interaction with my tired, worn-with-work, and thoroughly lonely mother. I drove carefully, but no sooner was I out on the most dismal and dangerous portion of Twenty-Ninth Street when a tire blew. The street was deserted except for a few drunken derelicts turned out from bars. They were crouched, tugging at their tattered coats and arranging newspapers, huddling in doorways for a meager allowance of warmth. I could taste my fear. Fantasizing Irish hyperbole, I thought it would be better to be mugged and beaten than to be late to pick up my mother. Maybe I would be lucky and be killed. This was just the situation that would render me anxiously fumbling for a good excuse while she fumed with rage. When facing disappointment, my mother was at her most dangerous and unpredictable wild self. It was at these inevitable, randomly occurring moments that my mother's disappointment and frustration with her lonely life broke down the love in her heart for me.

But there was hope. "Quickly, change the damn tire!" I ordered myself, swiveling my head both right and left, front and back. I was looking for menacing figures as if they would show themselves before I left the relative safety and warmth of the car. I popped the trunk, grabbed the bumper jack— surely an invention of a demented and sadistic devil posing as an engineer— ran around to the right rear tire, and placed it carefully. I frantically pumped the handle that immediately stuck to my ungloved hand from the cold. My breath frosted the air around the lug nut and froze my snot. The car was up. Run to the trunk, lift and roll the tire, throw it on, tighten the lug nuts, release the dangerously tilting bumper jack. *Swish*, no air in the spare!

Life is demanding. It requires energy and resources. I was found short. (After all, we are all short.) Now I would pay at the airport. When I finally arrived, my mother, always possessing an abundance of Irish whimsy and unpredictability, was sympathetic and loving. But at that moment, when the spare crumpled in the ice, I promised myself to always have air in my spare. I would learn that the only difference between pain and pleasure is how you see it, not what happens to you. I told myself I could not and would not even try to make up for what others were or what they did by being perfect. I would take full advantage of what my life had to offer. I would let those who are disagreeable beat themselves with their own anger, disgust, contempt, or rejection of me. In short, if I was doomed not to pay attention to the color of my socks, I would survive by enjoying my mistakes.

Where Did Anne Schultz Go?

I don't know for sure,
But I wanted her to live in a teacher's heaven,
For her view of me
Was—for my sad, lonely moments—a private haven.

I was a child who feared to read,
Who played at most a minor part in a smart and accomplished family.
I could not see in myself any seed
Of grace, of ease, of wit, of handsomeness—only desperate hope.

My family lived in remembrance
Of a time when a paternal light rained pleasure, company, and intellect
With profligate and steady remittance
On us, his sons, his bids on eternity, and his own *Abie's Irish Rose*.

When Dad's sun was set through consumptive disease,
The coldness of grasping attachment to what could have been
Descended like an ice age without comfort or ease.
It froze joy, stimulation, friends, yet left something awesome.

It left my mother and, by our closeness, my brother and me
A strong guiding North Star of love struggling for a fantasized grand future.
Such a gut-generated desire provided no sweet tea
Of relaxing passage of time, of comfort, friends, familial connection.

There I was at the beginning of adult life,

Faced with the certainty of my past and future failure in school.
Not reading produced confusion and strife.
I had an image of what I should, but was certain I could not be.

Ms. Schultz was a bird, intense while she focused
On social studies during the terror of the Second World War.
She "tremendjous" *tremendous* pronounced,
Chirped rapid-fire words and never seemed to alight.

My mother's struggling dream caused her to insist
That I take summer school to learn to type, which I did, on an old Royal.
Mother thought I read, as if her painful teaching must persist,
From many evenings stuffed with my mangling *The Adventures of Tom Sawyer.*

But typing I did, although I hardly knew
What the words I pecked out, with many strikeovers, meant.
My homework, fixed by Mom's slashing blue,
Caught Ms. Schultz's flighty attention simply because I typed.

Ms. Schultz blessed me with a compliment—
The first I had ever received from any schoolteacher—
She had not the slightest idea how much it meant.
She offered a possibility of learning; my lifelong flower bloomed.

We do not know what we are doing!
We cast about us those seeds, just so many words, and deeds.
What are we ending or beginning?
How sad, yet a chancy happenstance, we will never know.

Reflections on "Where Did Anne Schultz Go?"

Reflecting on what people do leads to some interesting questions. Anne Schultz led me to believe that I could learn from and emulate what I saw people doing. She gave me hope that I could graft the competence of others onto a growing repertoire of behaviors. I too could do things and enjoy accomplishing things. She said what I did in her class was worthwhile and interesting to her. After experiencing her opinion of me, I could decide what I am about and go after it. Moreover, I could hope to achieve my goals. I have, at various times throughout my life, actually thought I knew what I was about. By attending a whole host of motivational seminars, I dreamed of and conceived plans galore. Objectives were carefully set forth with the requisite deadline dates. They were obsessively sorted according to categories such as social, spiritual, professional, etc. Methods to achieve these usually too-ambitious goals were delineated. Even this book is a product of this effort.

Looking back on the last ten years, I see that despite my goals, my objectives, my process methodology—the meaning I inserted into my daily activity—there was an astonishing discrepancy. The gulf was between what I planned and what I actually did. Understand that I am not contending that these efforts were fruitless; it is just that they have borne a fruit I never knew existed or even could imagine or even could imagine I could imagine. Perhaps one of the most valuable by-products of these motivational seminars is that they led to a process by which I became aware of the massive and disturbing discrepancy between my past intention and my current achievement.

Before I lead you astray, I want to tell you that I am not disillusioned by these seminars. I have been in no way disappointed. One attendee pointed out to me that if you really learn—and remember, of course—one thing from each seminar, they are worth the expense and effort. What effort? They are, for the most part, entertainment. Both the leaders and attendees scintillate, in that the leaders seem to know and the attendees so earnestly want to know what the leaders think they should know. This fact says something profound about people. They have hope. They can comfortably conceive of others knowing more than they do. They have faith that such skills can be both communicated and learned. This pleasure is the rock-bottom, worst-case argument for the seminars.

Moreover, often these seminars are really useful to those of us who have not yet mastered life, which is all of us. And like a play by a master dramatist, they are usually an intense collation of the practical, the philosophical, the spiritual, and the vaguely imagined. Often they highlight what is important. They do excel in distilling in a short time almost all that is known about how to do something or other that can be taught. Sometimes they even help you decide what is worth trying to do. Imagine that what you want to do is get around a wall that must be climbed over. You place your almost-always overextended ladder against it. Puffing, you ascend. Getting to the top is what seminars teach. At the top, you recognize it was really some other wall you wanted to climb! How can you possibly lose if you get entertainment and a bouquet of wisdom from which you can choose whatever flower you wish to sniff?

What you do breaks down into a couple of domains. You say or do something. There is a whole host of things you intend. Sometimes that happens. However, lurking between these intentions are imaginable but unintentional results. These are like scattered sequins, only some of which shine and catch your eye. Then there are those other possible outcomes of totally unimagined sorts. They are cast about, but sometimes they are the processes that might fit the Buddhist aphorism that the teacher will appear when the student is ready to learn. Then it is magic time. We may think they are but minor gestures, polite, kind, thoughtful, disrespectful, sarcastic, disinterested, or otherwise, but those that become open to this communication may find them to be explosions of pain or pleasure. They sometimes provide the tracks for the train of our lives. That is what Anne Schultz, my high school teacher, did for me. I deeply regret I never told her what her passing compliment meant to me.

A Cemetery Is Forever, but Not Our Gifts

They are there forever, those cemeteries.
Yes, they change with time.
Everything slides, reaching for entropy,
Yet something of pattern forever remains.

Away with my grandson, chosen for untimely death;
Away with my father, my mother, my father-in-law.
Lost to the ground, into the ground, or into the fire,
They are swept into the cosmos from our home's hearth.

But is it ever the same after their disappearance?
The fact that we cannot distinguish what is left
Does not dictate that there is nothing still there
Of that sweet pattern, now only a fond remembrance.

It was a glorious evening
Splashed with color of early evening's sun.
Amid the distant sound of the surf,
I stood on the ground—nearby were
The graves of my long-lost and barely remembered father,
Of my vibrant, loving, but difficult mother.
Nearby my wife visited the grave of her father
Taken from us only a year or so ago.
A man, no surely a young man at eighty five.
How I hated to see him go!

My father lay against the piled-high white pillows.

Barely visible within the oxygen tent,
His darkly framed face, once fiery with charm and vibrancy, showed
Now pale and wan; it seemed to announce,
"I want to be a father to you but do not have the inspiration.
It was taken from me by this damned disease.
Remember, my little Al, what there is to remember,
Little in fact, because I am wasted,
But immense in loving with long-lasting intention."

My mother was sickly in pain and degrading disability.
She chain-smoked in her green chair, devouring books from the mobile library
Gaining on some lost possibility of a desired, enlightening education
That had bypassed her, leaving her talent, her strength barely cultivated.
She groused at me for my skimpy weekly visits.
I watched her vitality slip steadily away,
As her mood descended into consistent irascibility.
She was moving away from that passionate love for me,
Which still sustains me even in my darkest despair.
I remember her passion, her drive, her fierce Irish love
That all but destroyed me with its intensity, its inconsistency, and its whimsical aggression.

How I would welcome the challenge of trying with her once again
To gain that desirable, troubled communicative peace and confrontation of equals.

My father-in-law left us not unexpectedly.
A man of overwhelming giving, sprung from passivity and true affection,
This man showed me the charms of long life, of steady accomplishment,
Of deep love for what he was and what he could be.
He was a man of extraordinary ability who took me to his side
Like his own son. Fathering a son was something that life had denied him.
Being a father and feeling fathered bound us together in kindness and respect
But never seemed a fit subject to share openly.
It was always there, just under the surface of companionship,
Gaining assurance from my often imperfect but deep love for his Liz
And being shaped by conversational platitudes with golf, politics, and music.
It was there. We both knew it, but we never said it.

I moved quickly away from the graves and was misted by the damp salt airs.
I was escaping the gloom of all those things that could have been—that could
have been said.
I had not been man enough to create them, I think.
An old man's frightful and sobering thought, my spirit and soul still leak tears.
I had strewn a few fresh flowers on the grass,
Which would surely wilt after they slid from my slack hand.
I walked toward the car in the gathering darkness.
I glimpsed a gathering herd of deer in the car's glass.

I thought, *Next year I will be above these graves by the sea so awesome.*
With some heavy doubt about what form I would take,
Slowly I turned for a steady, last, open-eyed look.
A deer had begun quietly, quietly munching my gift, a fallen blossom.

My gift, vanishing only a brief moment after presentation,
Was but a weak and completely inadequate salutation.
The sly and quietly munching does and bucks seemed to declare:
    Now, do it now!
    Do it now always!
    Only now will it still quicken the quick!

Reflections on "A Cemetery's Forever, but Not Our Gifts"

Okay, so we know that Hogan could golf and that at one time he could box. George Archer saw another side of Hogan's creative genius one year while sitting with Hogan at a Masters' Champions Dinner:

> He came to the Masters' Champions Dinner the year after I won the Masters (in 1969). As defending champion, I got to do the seating arrangement and put Mr. Hogan right beside me. And I found out that night that Ben Hogan was a very good artist. He could draw horses with wings, dinosaurs—all kinds of mythical characters. He took a pen and he drew about four animals. I'm looking at this and I'm thinking, "God, if I had any nerve at all, I would get these things framed and have him sign them." But I was chicken. I didn't say anything and they just went in the laundry. Such detail, too. I sure wish I had taken them. I wish I had told the waiter, "I'll give you twenty bucks or whatever for those table cloths," but being young I didn't want to do something that was wrong at the Masters. (Mike Towle, *I Remember Ben Hogan*)

A CEMETERY IS FOREVER, BUT NOT OUR GIFTS

When I was young, time seemed to move slowly. Time seemed endless to me. It was full of promises: joy, ecstasy, sadness, boredom—in short, all the opposites that the spectrum of life choices offers every one of us. Those variegated events marched from the future into my present and instantaneously into the past at a slow, deliberate pace. What I failed to notice was that the pace of this transformation quickened ever so slightly each passing day. I am not sure when I noticed this ominous reality. Suddenly, time to do what I wanted to do was running out. At some point, this fact became part of my daily consciousness.

What was most disconcerting when I came to this realization was that while my list of things to be, to do, and to see lengthened, the number of my days shortened. I was stunned; I knew that I must pick and choose what was closest to my heart and mind. Bewildered, I wandered, lost and, sometimes, aimless amongst what was most important, most worthwhile, most pleasurable, most urgent, and most emergent. If I chose the most sensual, most entertaining, afterward I would think, *What is this? A day closer to death, yet no nearer to my loved family and friends, no nearer to being useful to the world.* If I chose action designed to lead to lofty and broad goals, a very important and oftentimes deluding part of my life, I reflected on and saw the disappointment on the faces of loved ones who so enjoyed my company but were deprived of my often clumsy but well-meaning companionship. Moreover, lofty goals, while they sounded the bell of peace and welfare, were more often than not fully outside my sphere of influence. My power seemed so puny, inadequate, and impotent. I mused that the world had such momentum and yet was so full of inertia; my capability to change things seemed ghostly or waiflike. If matters of urgency or emergency shattered my plans for the day, week, or month, I saw how out of control and unable I was even to stay focused on what I hadn't even chosen. What a feeling! This way of thinking made it so easy to blame the world and relieved me of any responsibility for my choices.

But then, what was I responsible for? Like an echo, a hard, trite, and truthful answer came to me: "Just do your best at each instant of time. Then you will have nothing to regret, not even when facing failure." Moreover, I could choose to make some small difference: a pat and smile to a friend in pain, a loan to a family member, an expression of gratitude to those who make my life a joy, a contribution to my strength of knowledge and will to sustain me through some battle in life that at any given moment I think worthwhile. I could make life a series of choices, such that I would never regret anything I did for myself and for others. Surely, it would never be enough. Just as surely it would often be misunderstood. But I still should be meticulously careful to follow the dictates of my best judgment, following the still and small quiet voice within. That way, when I and my loved ones pass, all of us would at least have a chance to come to the realization that after all, it was worthwhile. What better life could be imagined and lived?

Joy of Aging

For age has opportunity, no less
Than youth, though in another dress
And as the evening twilight fades away
The sky is filled with stars, invisible by day.
　　　　　　　　—Henry Wadsworth Longfellow

For me it was always true
That I knew what was what
When I was young.

Of course, you might be much wiser than I,
For you may have known
Even during the dangerous and daunting teenage years,
All along, that everything worthwhile is unknown
To any firm, certain, or practical extent.
I confess I did not.
I dove deep into concepts and experiences
With arrogant opportunism and ignorant optimism.
Without any soul-guiding gyroscope,
I thrashed around without a clue.
Oh, what there is to miss in life!
By being enthralled by the business of work,
By being obsessed by the one-eyed magic pleasure wand,
By being involved in what is right and just,
Rather than seeing, feeling, and thinking
　　　Just what is!
　　　Then doing!
Repeat ad lib.

Believe me.

I look back and down and all around with wonder,
Observing in the broadest sense
    Just what is.
Then like being struck by a triple lightning bolt,
I see, feel, and think; feel, think, and see; think, feel, and see
    Simultaneously.
I am stricken by this mighty triumvirate:
    The homogeneous,
    Orderless,
    Totally integrated—
    Seeing, feeling, thinking.

What a jazz!
From the scurrying spider faintly resembling a black widow,
To the charmed quark,
To the melding freedom and release of being in her,
To the sweetest of all threesome sensations:
    The knowing it will all be soon over,
    And I will return to the stars
    From whence I came.

    But surely I will be leaving my trace
    Here and there.
    God, I love it!
    I choose to go from this place of joy joyfully.

Reflections on "Joy of Aging"

For most of my life, I was certain that almost everyone knew more than I. My conviction was that others were better educated, more thoughtful, more wise, and without a doubt, more adept and more charming than I. I did not know how I came to that dismaying truth. A truth that has finally fallen away and decayed, I add with relief. I now have a rather vague but fairly accurate picture of both the how and the why of this dead belief's early development. I am now fairly certain that it is not always true. There is ample evidence in my life experiences to prove that there are many who surpass me in all the qualities mentioned above, yet I now know that many are not currently superior in any or all these characteristics. This later realization was no comfort to me. It simply forced me to be ever more selective in choosing from whom I borrowed templates for my life.

How did I come to this realization as I grew older? The answer is simple in words and difficult in practice. I watched and listened, and then I focused on the awareness of the emotional resonance of what I felt when I watched and listened. It is difficult enough just to watch and listen, but what required years of effort and practice was to ruthlessly cut my own experience and self-concept out of the things I saw, the things I heard, and the feelings I felt as a consequence. I was far from a natural. I still work at it on a daily basis. It is a truism that what I was, am, and will be need not be a part of what I understand. In fact, what I was, am, and will be are but an innate and intrusive barrier to my full pursuit of what is ongoing and is what I am trying to do at any given instant. That is paying mindful attention.

I had immense help from many of my teachers, from some books, and in my psychiatric training. But loving the process of learning awareness, kindness, and openness was a process that I could not master simply through education. It was like the difference between reading about the perfect golf swing and executing it or reading about blowing beautiful glass vases and doing it. The gulf between this understanding and practice is extremely wide, and the passage across is stormy. The massive effects from past personal storms are easy to manage. Oddly, it is the current subtle impacts of small tides and ripples of the past and distant storms that set me off course. They are hard to detect as feedback comes rarely and when one least expects it. While no longer a novice in this realm, I hope to remain a learner until I lose consciousness while dying.

One thing I have learned is that what I do not know is most often the most important and largest piece of life's puzzle. To place it in anywhere near the right part of the picture, I require self-awareness, kindness, openness, imagination, and courage. As a young man and a practicing physician, I suffered, as did so many of my patients, from the lack of these characteristics. I could have learned them at home had things been different. While there was kind intent in my early life, its practical application was sorely wanting. The only part of self-awareness in my homelife was an intimate knowledge of anger. Openness was only available in some expressions of physical affection. I take as my greatest personal accomplishment the building of my current skills in awareness, kindness, and openness. In that area, I was formerly deprived and dysfunctional. For whatever skills I currently possess, I owe thanks to those who have loved me despite my deficiencies. Without great strides in these areas, my life would have been handicapped, a failure, especially with my families. I have loved the process of learning awareness, kindness, and openness with great passion and joy, with considerable pain and anxiety, and with massive and sustained effort. It has and, I suspect, always will be my most profound and powerful pleasure.

Our Choice to Soar?

Old men, shoulders hunched, sitting on a porch,
Watch the sunset go from hot red to darkening glow.
Like aging biplanes perched nearby in a weedy runway,
Time slowly, surely, darkens their handheld torch.

They yearn to fly toward clouds and careless sky,
Dispersed into a space where they know they must go.
Part of their journey is unmeasured, undreamed, unknown.
They are musing, *Be something before I die.*

Languishing from a fading and failing will,
They have gradually slipped from youth to disuse.
The testicular juice, creating false hope of immortality,
Drains from them with an assist by dying.
Life deals them a poison pill.

Soft muscles mirror society's lack of meaning.
Some never knew it was they alone who must strive to soar.
The secret is that only they could find a soaring course
From their own awareness of impulses, thoughts, and acting.

Some choose nothing at all, no doubt a choice still.
Others hesitate, choose, and know not that they did so.
Even more are conscripted by a contemporary fad.
Only a fortunate few said, "It's *my god's* will."

They make an expansive statement,
Sound waves without echo.
Yet by their gods, some chose to act,
Which springs from spirit's enhancement.
    All will pass shoulders hunched from this scene;
    They sometimes surpass the common mean.

Reflections on "Our Choice to Soar?"

I ask for indulgence. I have written from a male perspective because I am a man. I believe the masculine point of view makes for a simpler statement for me in general. I think this poem applies to woman as well, but perhaps less accurately.

Aging attacks our strength, our will, and our joy. Only our strength and joy are a natural part of becoming old. In theory, joy should increase with age as depth and breadth of understanding substitute for intensity of physical pleasure. The shortening of the future and the lengthening of the past quench the fire of accomplishment. The content of our speech, especially when we are beleaguered by health problems, proportionately shifts from the future and present to the past as our past days grow more numerous and the available future days diminish. Thus, the "use it or lose it" coerced algorithm diminishes the set of our actions, leaving our life's playing field increasingly underused and neglected.

Regrets bred from passed-over opportunities are a variation of a road less traveled. Yet I assert that what we have viewed as unfortunate choices often lead to fresh personal vistas and insights. More often than not, our family and friends do not agree. We suspect, had we done this or that, we would have accomplished something that others would applaud. We might have left a mark before dying. But do we want to let others decide our value by how conforming to their own values our views and acts are? How much what we do brings in the marketplace? How noticed we are by society, or how much we change our culture? To do these things may be of value and, in themselves, may enhance opportunities. But do they sufficiently substitute for becoming what our light calls us to in our most inspiring dreams and brightest fantasies? These are what we should judge as enhancing our spirit.

In my view, it is better to do what I want than to be judged right and relevant by my peers. Admittedly, when society's accolades, money, or attention seem less than I think I deserve, it hurts. When that happens, I try to go inside to my private impulses, thoughts, and fantasies. It is there that I seek solace and contentment by musing that my judgment of the present and future is more important to me than the judgment of others of what I have done. It is even more important than being right, as the passage of time may brutally demonstrate to me. Not having the conceit to be certain I am right and making my own choices nevertheless leaves me feeling good. Following my own dreams and fantasies may make my life more of a struggle than leaving my choices to the whims of procrastination, society, or well-intentioned friends and relatives. I see this as my god's spirit.

Catch a Flying Dagger by the Hilt

When you ride in a boat and watch the shore, you might assume that the shore is moving. But when you keep your eyes closely on the boat, you can see that the boat moves. Similarly, if you examine many things with a confused mind, you might suppose that your mind and nature are permanent. But when you practice intimately and return to where you are, it will be clear that there is nothing that has unchanging self.

—Dogen

There is always what there is.
Beyond that is what we think there is.
Then we have many feeling overlays
Based on how we think life plays

That changes our personal goal.
Our ways of being take finite toll
On the human process, the way of the soul.

We decide where we should go
Feeling what happens: good, bad, or so-so,
Telling ourselves it is where we want to go.
     We think,
The world is supposed to turn our backs to the wind.
The world is supposed to halt cheek-puffing gusts.
The world is supposed to move us along our path.

Most imagine that would fulfill our fondest hopes.
Often we are mistaken when we grab for what we dreamed.
Often we are grief stricken when we get what our good seemed.
We curse our luck. "This is too hard or wretchedly occult."
We strive for our perceived good, but achieving it is difficult.
Through clenched teeth we say, "Oh, surely this won't do!"
Our human nexus, a flimsy superstructure, is brought low.

This is only decoration to what is.
What it does to us—is
Not what we thought it was.
Our view is but a human fantasy overly anthropomorphic.
If we just know what is beside us—that is phantasmagoric!

Or we lie back, passively thinking, *Soon I will react.*
That we think there is at times an illusion related to this fact.
Actually we think as if we were something separate.
Time and events march us, desperate or not.
When we are in there, it encircles us inexorably,
Whether or not we meet it reality-based and ably.
We often are surprised when we smack into what it is,
Every effort to avoid what is causes damages.
Putting aside conscious mind, overcome with feeling,
We are reactive, resisting, and reeling,

Or conversely, if what is is bolstering,
Then we could accept it—what is—and just be.

They are fortunate who see what is and what will be.
They seize that new being as suiting to a T.

What is becomes a part of them; they are completely homogeneous.
Then they are well melded to the world, no, the cosmos ingenious.
Like a well-oiled, intricate, and complex whirling device,
They have changed, integrated and dependent, willful, precise,

Bringing forth the human capability to cube myriad thoughts,
Bursting into bloom all human capability sans "oughts."
To construct, create, consecrate what needs be done just so—
Even sans borders, sans centers, it envelops all in holistic flow.
From threading the needle eye to the pole vault,
From loving action to sharp confrontation,
From reckoning a spacecraft's swift starlit path,
To the poet's twisted thought set straight to rhyme,
From sassy, tricky assay of Dow Jones's indexed fortune,
To free gifts of empathetic and sympathetic smiles.
This is a mix of the biologic integrated world.
This all is, with or without the labeling "good" or "bad."

This all is despite those humane appellations.
This all is ours to enjoy and engage.
All of us are empowered and impassioned
By the absences of narrow moral judgments.

After all, what there is is.
What there was, a certainty, is.
What will be, though largely unknown, it too is.
We will be part of its action, response, and reaction.
But more smooth, efficient, elegant without accretion.
Like rivers flowing,
Like white swans flying,
Like mongrels barking,
Like oceans' lapped roaring,
Like mounting, salty loving,
Enhancing or destroying, planned or unplanned,
It is what it is, though appreciation always helps,
And though thinking "good," "bad," or "even indifferent" doesn't.

A Bird on the Banister

I gaze through the French door
At a bird on the banister—
Nothing really sinister,
Sounding a rattling chirp.

He sings, he hops, I hope
Right 'n' wrong, good 'n' bad. Nope!

Feathered bantam blimp
Singing a song
For just that long.
Hmmm, hmmm, hmmm, hmmm.

Reflections on "Catch a Flying Dagger by the Hilt" and "A Bird on the Banister"

If you enjoyed "Catch a Flying Dagger by the Hilt" and if it gave you both pleasure and a confused feeling, please take the time to read it again.

> #224 Know How to Take Things
> Never against the grain, though they're handed to you that way. There are two sides to everything. If you grab the blade, the best things will do you harm; the most harmful will defend you if you seize it by the hilt. Many things that caused pain could have caused pleasure if only their advantages had been considered. There are always pros and cons; the trick lies in knowing how to turn things to your advantage. Things look different when seen in a different light. So look at them in the light of happiness. Don't confuse good and bad. This is why some people find contentment in everything, and others sorrow. This is a sure defense against the reversals of fortune, and a great rule for living, at all times and in every pursuit.
> (Baltasar Gracian y Morales)

The hardest thing in life is really seeing what is. Whatever we see, we think something about it, and what we see changes. That is the process: seeing something changes what is seen. Whatever we think about something we see, those thoughts generate feelings. Feelings then effect the change in what we see. What we think about something, rather than exactly what it is, is an aggregate of our life experience. Then we submit what we see to a rococo redesign, depending on what we hoped it would be. I wonder how we ever get anything right. Soon we are swamped by the hope that everything will end up the way we think we wanted it to be. We need help, and when we get it, it comes through some magical trick of fate. Our fate reworks our soul. It is wearing.

What really boggles our process and eventually effects our goals is that we sincerely believe that the world should support us. We come to think that what happens to us is not just some minute part of a great mystical and largely unknown machine. Rather, we actually believe the cosmos must be concerned with how we feel, what we think, and what we are doing. This is too much for most of us; it is for me. When surprised by the way the cosmic ball has bounced, we turn for guidance to a god, a king, a president, a hero, an antihero, or anybody else whom we can deceive ourselves into thinking knows better than we do. If we could just accept that we know next to nothing and allow ourselves to be open and accepting, what is happening around us can be perceived. No one I have known or know of is any better off than the rest of us in this matter, nor do I think some all-knowing messiah is about to burst onto the temporal horizon—not that there is any lack of those who proclaim they know what is what. Watch them: some are lucky, some unlucky, but none of them know. Given that immutable and everlasting fact, we might as well bungle through everything entirely on our own.

We bemoan our fate, not realizing it is fate that teaches us how to live and, eventually, how to die. Admittedly, I find it just as hard as most of you do, but I think it an intriguing, engaging, and enthralling game. What is odd is that we often fall into the classical error of thinking all this has anything directly to do with being human. Rather, what is *is* about the cosmos and its myriad, squared, interacting facets and intricacies.

Another classical error is to accept what seems as inevitable, immutable, relentless, and ineluctable. What we forget is this: Though we are possessed of only a minuscule capability to change things, that tiny capability is an essential part not only of our humanity but of our biology and the very workings of the cosmos. In short, the cosmos depends on us, not just to mess things up but to put things right. We are not just predetermined reactors to the events of the cosmos. I think we need to get busy. I have an intuition that there is not that much time left, considering what we know about our and the cosmos' evolution. We are the agents of evolution though our culture.

Every attempt to turn our back on our place in the cosmos or to act as if we are more than we are inflicts injury on us. Every attempt to shift our individual or collective responsibility delays the process and inflicts pain on our fragile but still marvelous bodies, our ego functions, our enduring spirit, our body politic, and our bewildering cultures. All evasions are fantasies of denial, yet they too are an essential part and parcel of the forever integrated cosmic nexus. So we must move to accept and act to change it; that is our biological imperative.

Then there is the nasty, naive, and juvenile habit of labeling things *good*, *bad*, or *indifferent*. Some things are to be despised and resisted, some to be embraced and assisted, and some to be dodged and left to lie dormant. But it is the essence of humanity that all must be engaged, seen for what they are, and changed through our acts, our will. How do you know what is good or bad? How often have you feared something that turned out to be a blessing? How often have you desired something that turned out to be repulsive and devastating? It is what you think the outcome is that determines whether you resist, encourage, or ignore. But labeling *good*, *bad*, or *indifferent* is of no help at all in knowing how to effect change in the cosmos' course. It is only what is that is a help in determining the process and outcome. How elegant is this capacity to be integral and a participant part of what we are acting on when we *are* clearly what it *is*. There is no separation between us and what happens that we are perceiving. Such a synthesis is so beautiful; we soar. We are alive when being so entwined, engaged, appreciating—rather than judging and thus dividing—being a part of what we are doing makes us feel vibrant and capable of meeting the challenge of humanity's expectations! That is the purpose in ongoing life.

The One Who Is Good at Shooting

The one who is good at shooting does not hit the center of the target.

—Zen saying

There is no center.
No matter how well you aim, the center eludes you.
A whirlpool concept to enter,
And then you profoundly lose yourself too.

Falling from certainty,
You take your best aim and immerse yourself in it.
To be near racks creativity,
The center abruptly veers, demanding all your wit.

Wisdom hunts perfection.
The you who is good at shooting knows you have, at best, a near miss—
Even with faultless technique and exact execution.
Eventual and total success you choose reluctantly to dismiss.

It is inaccuracy
That you shave away to reduce to an absolute minimum.
Engorged through effort of missing leads to ecstasy.
Acceptance of error creates an almost orgiastic residuum,
    Enlivened and inflamed from everlasting seeking.

Reflections on "The One Who Is Good at Shooting"

The nature of God is a circle of which the center is everywhere and
the circumference is nowhere.

—Empedocles

The Heisenberg principle and chaos theory spelled the end to scientific certainty, particularly to clear and accurate measurement. According to the Heisenberg, the method one chooses to gather data alters the values of the measurement and confounds an arrow's flight. For instance, pulling electrons by means of a static charge changes the mass of the electron one is measuring. Measuring the location of the electron changes its location. Similarly, an arrow conforms to chaos theory. It predicts that performing a mathematical or geometric exercise repeatedly, even if performed with identical methods, does not always lead to the same answer. For instance, if you were on the sun and could view the coast of England, you could measure its linear circumference. If you were to view the English coast from the moon, performing the same type of measurements, you would find a higher value, because you could see more indentations of the landmass. If you were to view it from near space, your answer would be yet higher, again for the same reason. If you descended to Earth and paced off the shoreline, again the value would be much larger. If you then inspected the entire shoreline with a magnifying lens, the value would be still larger. If you measured the shoreline using an electron microscope, the length of the circumference would be near infinite. Chaos theory predicts that the flap of a butterfly wing in Japan will modulate the weather in New York, but not always in the same way. What do these facts have to do with shooting an arrow at a target? What is their impact on our emotions?

What we can gleam from the arrow's flight is that the center of the target is an illusion; it cannot be precisely pierced. No matter how much you practice, how skillfully you draw the bow, or how acute your aim is, the center is simply not there no matter where you strike the target. Yet you try to achieve the unachievable. Trying racks your brain, entices your interest, and is profligate with your money. Lessons, books, exercises, trainings, and even the mysteries of Zen understanding, if there is such a thing, help one approach the center that is not there. The contemplation of this process yields immense frustration. It also engenders an acceptance in the master, leading to ever more accuracy.

Awareness that one cannot succeed does not frustrate a master. The process of achieving what is possible is fascinating and pulls at one's heartstrings. Inevitable failure to achieve the specific goal yields to the pleasure of seeing how close one can get. It is the essence of beauty: these thoughts, these emotions, and these drives and wishes expressed through behavior. These engender a blissful state of intense engagement and sensual satisfaction in which time shrinks to the passing instant and blends with the future.

God, the Other Face of Doubt

When life starts to slide away from you,
Austere realities collide with your hopes.
The pain of disappointment wrenches—
You could choose to face fragility.

So comforting is the proffered vision
Of everlasting embodiment!
An anodyne of supreme power—
Easygoing but way beyond proof.

On the other hand, what if you turn away?
Encounter the other face of doubt.
One truth in an unembodied God—
No, you as you in eternity!

There is certain peace in knowing that
You must express your life:
Let fly in the universe
What you have become through what you do.

Each single breath, with or without sighs,
Expands in evermore minute real rings;
To the points, curves, and corners of the cosmos,
They embrace everything while passing.

Whenever close up and near to you,

Where they can detect your more dense scent,
The vapor that only you created
Is a brawny mutating event.

Choose to be sure: your goal is clearly humane.
Choose to be sure: your process is crystal pure.
Choose to be sure: you are what you can become.
Choose to be sure: your doing is what you meant.

Reflections on
"God, the Other Face of Doubt"

I cannot recall when I started to think about my decline. I cannot recall what my first thoughts were. I cannot exactly recall what I felt like after thinking these first thoughts about my own death. As best I can remember, I was about forty-nine. I had resigned from my teaching post at the university. My wife and I bought a luxury thirty-five-foot fifth wheel and a huge truck to drag it. At Christmas, we embarked on our first trip. We went to Pacific Grove, California. After parking this behemoth, we settled into a weeklong leisurely vacation. Soon my wife fell ill with the flu; she suffered severe malaise and high fever. Within three days, I felt the first symptoms of the same illness. I was so sick it seemed that my only hope of survival was to die. I watched our pleasure in the vacation on the Monterey Peninsula take wing and our Christmas at home scrubbed. My equanimity evaporated when I remembered I had overlooked renewing our medical insurance. When the owner of the trailer park ordered me to move the fifth wheel to another berth, my weakened state made this minor task a monumental obstacle. With an abundance of curses and bathed in sweat, I relocated the truck and fifth wheel. I was so sick that I feared I would die while reconnecting the sewer pipe to the toilet outlet.

I had started our new venture in trailer life elated to be free of the endless fatiguing politics and fear-engendered lassitude that gripped my department of psychiatry at the university. I had brought a pile of books to devour and fine music to enjoy. My wife planned dinners out at the best restaurants. I had looked forward to spending time with my surrogate father, Leland Long, my father-in-law. He was always more kind to me than I deserved and, almost without exception, a congenial, intelligent companion. I was thrilled to think of the soothing comfort and powerful beauty of the sea, of the walks on the strand while being misted by the early morning fog, of the vistas of pastel-colored sunsets and twilights, and of the distant, rhythmic, murmuring surf to ease me into peaceful slumbers and rejuvenating dreams. A flu virus causing fear for both of us wiped these delightful prospects from my mind. An austere reality had collided with my expectations. I started to look into the face of my decline. I felt the absence of pleasure. I anticipated coursing through a future of always diminishing expectations. Then I did not know how long "long-term" would be—a week or twenty years? I am still working on this understanding.

Throughout my childhood, I had been told of the certainty of a heavenly future after death. My mother, deeply attached and forever grieving for my father from the time I was six until her death thirty years later, often fondly caressed the frame of his picture on the mantel. She mused, *I will be with him. I will see him again.* She never spoke of the joy of living, but did speak of the hope of seeing him again. After his death, she did laugh, dance, joke, and fume with Irish intensity but only when caught unawares by life's pleasures. My point is that one of her messages was this: There is another world after this life that is much like life on earth, but in a place where people are physically disembodied and stripped of pain, malice, impatience, revenge, nastiness, and longing for solitude. They definitely do not pick their noses. They live there forever enjoying and will be forever close to their loved ones who are destined to join them at a later time. I never really believed this fairy tale, but it was still a real comfort. My mother must know these things. Such assurance was similar to my naive belief at six that my father might not die. As he was a doctor, he should be able to cure himself. I wondered why he had not cured himself. I had hope, but there was still my hope he would miraculously wake. Even his postmortem sighing seemed the sound of life coming from his medical shroud, his oxygen tent. I excitedly told my mother that he was still alive. I grabbed her hand and tried to drag her into his room.

After a prolonged and dangerous brush with becoming a fundamentalist minister—a plan that my mother was unkind enough to ridicule—I became, as a teenager, an obnoxious and argumentative atheist. Two of my closest college female friends practicing a fiery brand of Baptist conviction argued with me in hopes of converting me to their fold. I wonder where they are now. Had they offered lovemaking, they would have improved their chances of success. My beliefs reflected the ambience of my relationships. This was a fact of my early life at home in the isolation of my mother's society and continued on into my early years at college. When I began college at sixteen, the contradiction of being an atheist and believing I'd see my father and mother in the afterlife did not bother me. I breezed by that I firmly believed in a heavenly paradise in which I could get to know my long-dead and almost unknown-to-me father.

I was practicing psychiatry in Orange County, California, years after my mother died. A fellow resident, a practicing Jew, subleased a room in my office suite. We had argued frequently when we had worked together as residents, but we had made an uneasy peace when we shared space. A fond acquaintance developed. He was in a training analysis, seeing his analyst four times per week. One day he did not return to our offices after his analytic session. I never saw him again. He was struck down by an acute attack of pancreatitis that rapidly became peritonitis and, soon after, gas gangrene. In a pressurized chamber, he lingered in agony for almost three months. I suffered from regret that I had not tried to be closer to him, as he was enough like me in interests and intensity in his personal opinions to annoy me, and therefore a friendship would have been interesting and challenging. Near the end of his life, I called the hospital to arrange a visit. I hoped to force a visit by exercising my medical privilege and, thus, be able to say good-bye. But the nurse adamantly refused me. She said with obvious sadness that I would not even recognize him, that he was intensely repulsive in appearance, and that he was in a deep coma. He would not be aware of my visit. I did not force the issue. I currently believe this was a failure of courage. I did go to his reform Jewish funeral.

On the side of the grave opposite where the other mourners and I were standing, his wife and five children lined up, looking down as they lowered the casket into the grave. The rabbi explained that Judaism believes that what one has done in life is the only part of you that will live forever. I never forgot those words. I took them as an admonition. Further, his words confronted my ill-formed belief that I would see and be with my father and mother after my death.

Through the choices we make, we affect most those people and things that are close to us. Simply by living our path, we affect absolutely everything in the universe for an eternity. This realization can be depressing or liberating depending on whether we decide to choose consciously your life path. Whether deliberately chosen or not, what we do is always of consequence.

Choosing Life with Fire

Don't miss the pieces of life you want,
Or death will come to you with a card dealer's taunt.
He will embrace your time with a lover's eager grace,
Then you can acquiesce to that which all of us face.

As it has always been, life's course is but finite choices.
Bring from your quiet considered fantasies strong voices
Asking, even demanding, of life's raw exigencies.
All we can envision and act on, take firm stances.

From the ovaries' oversupply of ovum,
Few are selected for an animated freedom.
The mind, ladened with free and formless visions,
Drafts plans, setting forth requisite conditions.

Only one of many, the fertilized egg, a single selection,
Grows though injury to gastrula from sperm penetration,
To fetus, to a squalling but mostly cooing newborn.
From passion, love, at times hate, it grows to a life unknown.

Like our choices,
A babe owns only an unknown but fixed future, a truism beyond the
commonplace,
A transformation of many mirrored fantasies focused on one point and place
Seize from time-bound seriatim set, enfold one element in vibrant fond
embrace.

You may give them the light of the sun's day.

Do not shirk from sweat or pain of failure!
It is a given that loss may be your only pay.

Fear of pain, time dissipated, energy drained
Are life's abortions. A life not amply lived.
Fear more death, always smiling, taunting;
Due to inaction, you cashiered life's wanting.

Though not without some threat of nocturnal regret,
With hardy and bold action,
May you dream dreams burning lustrous.
Genius is but for the few.
Others may not be warmed
By your favorite fire,
But even so, you could gaze
Quiet at what we all face,
And know, "I lived—choosing a life with fire."

Reflections on
"Choosing Life with Fire"

> *This is the true joy in life, the being used for a purpose recognized*
> *by yourself as a mighty one; the being thoroughly worn out before*
> *you are thrown on the scrap heap; the being a force of Nature*
> *instead of a feverish selfish little clod of ailments and grievances*
> *complaining that the world will not devote itself to making*
> *you happy.*
>
> —George Bernard Shaw

Most of us are fortunate. We are born with a smorgasbord of dreams, fantasies, and capabilities. We can be satiated by any one of an almost infinite variety of life's tasty morsels. A few of us are left out of these choices due to genetic error, poor endowment, or crippling perinatal accidents. As soon as we are born, we begin to eat the leaf of life. We are like the voracious larva of the monarch butterfly. He consumes twenty-seven hundred times his weight before he turns into a butterfly and begins his first flutters, the first inches of his twelve-hundred-mile migration from Colorado to Santa Cruz, California. He sheds his great vegetarian weight, becoming gossamer in stuttering flight. But the temperature must be right in excess of fifty-five degrees, and the winds, light.

There was a gifted and skilled artist, a sculptor. His specialty was huge solid-stone elephants. They were so elephant-like that they put the king, his patron, in a state of awe. One day, while gazing in amazement at a work in progress, the king wondered how this man shaped stone into what seemed to be the essence of all the elephants in the world. It was an unlikely eventuality that granite would shed its angularity into the smooth, folded, imperfect in form but perfect likeness in the spirit of these great beasts. He asked the sculptor, "How do you do this?" The artist, a man of few words, at first replied, "I do not know, but I will think on it." The artist said no more for many days. After a long time, he asked for a hearing with the king. After respectfully greeting his monarch, the sculptor answered as if it were still the same conversation. "I sit and look at the stone. I walk around the stone and gaze at it. I close my eyes and see the stone as it is. I touch my cheek to its coldness in the night. I warm my hands on it when it is sunny. I rub water on it. I sleep near it. I caress it, for I have grown to love it. I do nothing to change the great stone until I clearly see the elephant within it. Then I carve away everything in the stone that is not elephant. Only then have I created my vision of an elephant."

So there we are, fresh from the womb, wet with amniotic fluid, and bloody. Expelled from maternal nirvana by the action of hormones, muscle, and the intervention of benign abetting instruments—the doctors and nurses. Cuddled and nursed, we express our need for satisfaction by sucking and our annoyance by crying. Immediately all that is not us is beginning to be carved away, at first by family, then by the exigencies of life: politics, circumstance, culture, mores, chance. Our smorgasbord of realizable dreams, fantasies, and skills shrinks and continues to do so until the ultimate implosion—death. This sounds vaguely depressing. What is missing?

Choice of course. We need to watch out if we choose something. There just might be enough left of the smorgasbord that you will get it. Then what do you do with it? How can you enjoy misfortune, which is part and parcel of the choices? How can you not be saddened by the pleasure that you know is soon going to pass? How can you know what you can choose from, since you don't know exactly what is within you? As the artist said, see, feel, absorb, and make a choice by carving off what is not you. Then you will be the essence of the you that you could not even at first imagine.

Section II

From Within: Our Defense

A Giant Leaping from between Our Eyes

What comes from inside?
Giants leaping from between our eyes!
A force waxing and waning, a tide
That often shows our desired selves—as lies.

"An eye for an eye,"
Taught from Mother's lap, "A tooth for a tooth."
Knots of self-will, malice, envy, a lie,
Blood-brewed error from Father's hand, a man-fashioned truth.

Primitive and hard,
Power grows lusty, the self to glorify.
Casting shadowy acts against lives scarred.
Self-same stimulus to other meanings may testify.

Phoenix feelings fly
From life scarred from the same facts of shadows
Earlier risen to a piercing pitch to terrify.
Now from all in one, one in all blooms in heaven's meadows.

"One in all, all one"
Defines dyadic acts as partnership.
Like boys teeter-tottering, growing through fun,
May it blossom into every point of the universe's tip.

That affinity is connectedness:

Harm to me, harm to you.
Harm to us, harm to them.
Harm to you, harm to me.
Harm to them, harm to us.

Love is structure and connection lacking self-will
That, when passing to eternity, leaves no unpaid bill.

Reflections on
"A Giant Leaping from between Our Eyes"

"Like a ball batted back and forth," says an ancient text, The
Yogabindu Upanishad, *"a human being is batted by two forces
within; one, the upward drive to evolve into spiritual beings;
the other, the fierce downward thrust of our past conditioning as
separate, self-oriented, physical creatures."*
—From *Conquest of Mind* by Eknath Easwaran

Human acts and their accompanying thoughts—which in turn engender
feelings—could be divided into two categories: those acts that serve the
self and those that serve the cosmos. Normally we see the former as selfish
(therefore bad) and the latter as humane, advancing the consciousness of the
cosmos (therefore good). I propose that only those acts that are good for the
self (therefore selfish) can be humane. The reason is that if we mistreat or
damage the self, we are damaging a finite and important, though very small,
part of the cosmos—ourselves. We have the right to strive to achieve what
we perceive as benefiting ourselves. Our basic and innate nature is aligned
so that we act to enhance the connectivity of the entire cosmos. If we are
reasonably close to our natural potential, this is the guiding algorithm of our
lives. This is a type of biological intent we plan, though it is rarely the result
we are looking for due to the impact of socialization.

Each of our acts fits into an outlandish but seamless mosaic of the
inevitable, halting yet always advancing evolution of the cosmos. How our
acts fit evolution can best be understood by picturing one of those strange
geometries advanced by modern physicists and mathematicians. All our
acts can be plotted on some bizarre hyperspace figure with no borders, no
sides, and with continuous and fluid surfaces. Each act, a point, must be
related to every other, like all the points on an imaginary antiballoon. As

these acts multiply, they remain always interactive and complementary. They are products of our own mind, yet each has a variable transformation in space and time. That is, at one instant, a given act means one thing, at another instant, still another. This variability is a measure of the difference between our conscious and unconscious intent and the process course of the acts' points. Thus, we hold an intent, which we are more often than not incapable of presenting with any specific truth or accuracy. The reason for this lack of truth is that what we intend must comply with the dictates of our self-image even though we are never fully aware of all the features of that image. We can, however, approach ever closer to that awareness of self and thus diminish the deleterious effects of unintended outcomes that seem so bad to an imagined godlike observer. This asymptotic approach—that is, approaching but never reaching some ideal—to self-awareness is an invariant obligation of all people.

Lost Doors

When Jigoro Kano, the founder of judo, was quite old and close to death, the story goes, he called his students around him and told them he wanted to be buried in his white belt. What a touching story; how humble of the world's highest-ranking judoist in his last days to ask for the emblem of the beginner! But Kano's request, I eventually realized, was less humility than realism. At the moment of death, the ultimate transformation, we are all white belts. And if death makes beginners of us, so does life—again and again. In the master's secret mirror, even at the moment of highest renown and accomplishment, there is an image of the newest student in class, eager for knowledge, willing to play the fool. And for all who walk the path of mastery, however far that journey has progressed, Kano's request becomes a lingering question, an ever-new challenge:

"Are you willing to wear your white belt?"
—*Mastery* by George Leonard

Life moves from infancy
Steadfastly offering only a choice.
Nothing but an entrance to life's fancy
And that, forced by the gravity of Mother's need.

Soon things are looking up for individuation,
As flopping about changes gradually to crying or gurgling—
Only to meet the unexpected—parent's prohibition,
Which springs from breast, warmth, and things above.

With no doors and only shadowy figures

From a wending and winding hallway,
With the rushing days, the detail triggers
The picture of people this way and that way, pointing.

Demanding, showing, explaining, exclaiming.
"Open it, this is your lost door, your longed-for way."
These are the important people in your living!
They proclaim, plead that they really know
    The choices you should make,
    The routes you should take.

Remember that the lost door closes,
And it locks forever shut
Behind you. In a terrifying short time, losses
Gather, not to be daunted
    By the new hallway,
    Which is now your way.

Again new figures loom pointing,
Again you choose or not, for fate dictates.
You must be on your way, following
Ultimately only through your choices.
    The others are pointing.
    They too must choose
    Their own lost doors
    By helping you choose yours.

Beginnings

When you come to the end of the beginnings,
The notion comes to you
That life has been like a baseball game—innings
Endured to the final score.

More often than not, we have struck out
Like home-run stars: Ruth, Souza, Maguire,
Air-squashing swings that are so stout
Do nothing less than cause us to look the fool.

It is a burden to those serious-minded
That we often seem so stolidly and awkwardly inept.
Macho, I kissed her in the dark—"love mended."
I thought her squirming, passion. But I trod her toe.

While laughable, it is necessary to be such a fool.
Yet through this awkwardness, we enter the only wayward door
Where we can embrace adventure—the only tool
For life, a field strewn mostly with ashes and a few rare gems.

How can we soften that hard embrace:
The chasm between what we are and what we could be.
On both sides, a faint and foggy trace.
Between that, the broad cleft of our nakedness.

It is our willingness to open the lost door,

Yet to view what we have been.
Unblinking, we must discern yet love our lore
Of what is against what we could choose to be.
    Bravely open the lost door.
    Be exactly the fool you are.

Reflections on
"Lost Doors" and "Beginnings"
Paired Poems

Each of us has a task in life; it is to move in some direction. The goal is to proceed on a branching path that makes us everything we can be. Yet as I see it, there is no end, no achievement, no object, no rainbow at the end of this golden path. In short, there is no real "goal" in the usual sense of the word. All there is is the end of beginnings. Each move in some direction is a choice. If we do not overtly act, it is still a choice as it eliminates other acts that could occur. Once the choice is made, it is irretrievable. And these choices are grave ones. They stamp the character of our lives. The way we play the game is to make choices in the right way, even if they have tragic consequences. What in the world is the right way? That is what we learn in the calculus of life.

We can keep making the same choices over and over—the theme of most lives. The same choice, the same path, the same result. The result that matters to us is how we feel on that path. When making those choices, the information available for our understanding of the consequences is always meager, inaccurate, vague, unreliable, and insufficient. It is almost as if these choices are rushing toward us as the galaxies swish by a spaceship leaping to light velocity in a science-fiction movie. Choices keep coming. No matter how we lust to have more time and more information to put these things together before we open the door of our choice, the other available doors simply keep offering themselves. Although the knowledge that they will immediately close after we pass through is frightening, we still must open them to live. After all, what other metachoices do we have? Only death, sometimes coerced, but an advertent or, most often, inadvertent ultimate choice evolves naturally from a lifestyle. Eric Berne, MD, said something like a man chooses how to live, and he also chooses how to die. It is the inevitable last beginning.

Even though we must always make choices with inadequate information and without being certain of where those choices will ultimately lead, there are guideposts. The guideposts point a way, but to what effect in our lives? There are books, plays, television, movies, and most powerfully, people in our lives. These point out a way of being what and who they are, letting us know what happened and what the thoughts and feelings generated by the happening are. Besides being examples provided gratuitously or by request, they offer advice. People in our lives are involved by being in love with us, which means suffering when we suffer, enjoying when we enjoy, or sometimes, surprisingly, by being detached. Being detached preserves the loved one's autonomous self and respects their integrity. As a consequence, loving sometimes requires us to forgo the expression of closely held opinion, advice, criticism, confrontation, and especially interference. Being detached manifests love by showing respect for the choices of others, though not necessarily agreement. Letting the loved one act in a way we think is wrong can be a powerful test of our love.

Detachment can go too far. For instance, a serious charge is brought against a lawyer's client. The potential sentence is lifelong. The defendant is anxious; the lawyer confident. The trial nears its last few hours, and the jury will return a verdict at eleven. The defendant becomes increasingly fearful. He remonstrates, "What if I am found guilty?" The lawyer answers, "You won't." "But what if I am?" The clock strikes eleven. They both take note. The lawyer turns to look at him with clear, cold eyes. "I go to lunch, you go to prison." Be wary of those who will not suffer and share joy with you. It is hard enough for those who love you to tell you the truth and not manipulate you. What chance do you have with those who don't love you or just need you?

So what is the right way to make choices? How I wish I could find a satisfactory answer to this question for myself. I don't know much, but what I know has to do with being what Jews mean when they say, "He's a mensch!" It does not mean he is right, wrong, smart, informed, even well-meaning, or particularly effective, just that he is a human being. My choice is this path. My suggestions appear grossly inadequate to the mystery these poems and reflections encompass, but realizing this inadequacy is a consequence of my choice to be a mensch.

Our Goal: Amplify, Amplify

> *Our lives are frittered away by detail.*
> *Simplify, simplify.*
>> —Henry David Thoreau

> *Exercising our will is what we are.*
> *Amplify, amplify.*
>> —Albert Globus

Speaking to Henry:
We know and accepted what you are claiming,
Even as we imagine in a still larger sense:
"Obviously it is not all there is to our being."
Amplifying our inner and outer search is our essence.
This process poses puzzling questions—and ever
By volition, we set forth chameleon answers.

You are my favorite crank, Henry Thoreau,
Your content is so painfully convincing,
But when I heard your work carefully read through,
You sounded fussy, judgmental, and carping.

Your backwoods approach in classic inquiry
Made me wonder if what we were all about
Was not worth your drawn-out and rejecting query.
But your point had penetrating, no-nonsense clout.

Simplify, simplify—

To set aside the hurly-burly of contemporaries,
To see closely and carefully all irreducible minimum,
To focus life on what could pass muster in a clear mind's eyes,
To forge meaning on the requisite grind of life's continuum.

You spun ideas from a sparseness that assassinates sanity.
You were doctrinaire, dogmatic, and apostolic.
Your approach demanded friendship with one's own spirit
And was only for those with fondness for self-inspired intellect.

Your ideas speak to us from a historical time of intense labor,
When man burned the flesh of life against time and elements.
Now there is more energy, time, range, depth to fully savor.
Imagine what we could do with so few impediments!

Unfortunately *could* is the operative word.
For most of us blindly dodge our current birthright,
Leaving our very existence up to a merciless sword:
Lack of care. We could have had expanding personal light!

All we need do, with our mind's play,
Is to have the courage to plow ahead,
To seize what awaits us every single day—
Not recoil from our glorious fate instead.

With our newborn, astonishing technological prowess,
We could enlighten and irradiate emotion with thought,
A heady mixture—intoxicating life—we may caress
With a loving and knowing embrace, though by necessity taught.

It demands spirit and boldness, all remakes
Of our power and our beauty, assuredly to ascertain,
And the courage to dodge our potential futures' mistakes.
Committing a tragic sin, to hold back, could remain.

We must recognize and embrace our beauty,

Our power,
Our godlike stature.
No matter how afraid, we can step forward,
Heart ahead of head,
Thought awash in feeling,
Feeling awash in thought.

To live our mistakes but still to know,
Our spirit may—must—certainly grow
On a tangled pathway unknown
With an entirely new spirit sown.

Turn from the fearsome past.
Put aside all doubt, as we are awesome.
Now it is ours firmly to attest.
Imagine what can be willed to come.

Reflections on "Our Goal: Amplify, Amplify"

We have stood on the shoulders of those who have come before. More often than not, it has not been a voluntary lift. Much of human progress, which has led to leisure and our capacity to philosophize, has been coerced from the pliable and grudging but all too passive masses. Those who did the coercing planned and aimed to achieve their own and their progeny's benefit. What they accomplished through forcing others into involuntary servitude surprisingly served to benefit all people. Here I am not referring only to slavery but to those who worked their lives away in hopes of gaining reasonable subsistence or even riches. More often than not, their labor was hard, unremitting, and filled with mind-numbing drudgery. For most of history, even subsistence was a forlorn hope, quashed at the whim of those in power through the manipulation of wealth or by those merely willful and cruel. This manipulation and cruelty is aimed at perpetuating the exercise of power. It was not difficult to maintain this type of control, up to about five thousand years ago. It was less simple starting in the Renaissance about six hundred years ago. It has been only recently, perhaps beginning with public education, that the life goals of those in power became harder and harder and maybe impossible to achieve. With the arrival of the information age, it has, fortunately, become next to impossible for any oligarchy to deprive people of their birthright, not that they do not try. But apparently, their task has become unmanageable through the growth of limited democracy and egalitarianism based on capability. Humankind's consciousness has passed the first few seconds of a new "big bang." It flies to every conceivable corner of what is philosophically, spiritually, intellectually, and physically possible.

So you think I have run off the tracks of reality and sensibility! Not at all. Now all can learn. All can find out. Everything is possible for the man or woman who can both look inward and outward, bravely seeking reality-based truth. The tools of the information age are now cheaper and less perishable than food. Knowledge can flow everywhere and at any time. At the same time, since Freud's pioneering exploration and recent strides in the techniques of psychotherapy, the means of correcting the inevitable and common errors in the social aspects of parenting are available to all, especially those with the commitment and personal power to seek them out.

Oddly, at this point in history there is, in the name of mistaken economy and practicality, a serious but ill-planned public disinformation program. It is aimed at ridiculing into nonexistence a recent powerful development of the twentieth century: the contemporary modes of psychotherapy. I cannot say for certain why psychotherapy is ridiculed and undervalued. I suspect the motivation for such a regressive move comes from a deep and unhappy truth that cannot be comfortably accepted. Psychotherapy makes undeniable the fact that even the most powerful, most effective, and most adept of us can benefit from the intervention of a therapist. Particularly galling to our self-esteem is to accept the truth that sometimes the therapist who *can* help us is even less competent than we are. If this were not the case, Tiger Woods would not need Butch Harmon, his coach and teacher, or someone just like him. I daresay the most adept coach cannot outperform his best and more advanced students or clients. Aren't we being arrogant when we claim we need competent, empathetic, and sympathetic coaches and consultants for all our endeavors but not for personality retooling? Please! No digging around our secret world of personality. That's off-limits?

Yet psychotherapy, in its many and various forms, is a discipline that grows daily in content, in effectiveness, and in technical expertise. It is available for a modest sum: less than what it costs to buy a new car, to have a face-lift and a tummy tuck, or to have the front yard landscaped. While not always successful, there is little loss in trying psychotherapy several times over. After all, the process itself, except in the hands of the incompetent therapist, is normally not all that unpleasant. Trying at least gives you the possibility of achieving your potential. That is amplifying what you are to approximate what you could be.

Wherefore, in, of, and from Are You, My Unconscious?

"Unconscious" *is defined in* Webster's Ninth New Collegiate Dictionary: *"The part of the psychic apparatus that does not ordinarily enter the individual's awareness and that is manifested especially by slips of the tongue or dissociated acts or in dreams."*

Similarly, I can report from my own small experience that the unconscious is exquisitely beautiful, the very source of beauty. And it is orderly; it can be traveled. My own travel in the unconscious has been systematically, carefully planned. We can all go there and come back, bringing with us a wealth of understanding which we can use for enriching life.
                    —From *Conquest Of Mind* by Eknath Easwaran

Inspired by Shakespeare's *The Tempest*: "I wake and cry to dream again."

We all go there through all our years.
    Sometimes we know it,
    And sometimes we don't.
When we like being there, it disappears.

When we are not there, there it surely is.
Whether we know it or not, there we are.
When we are there, it is not.
When we think of being there, it flies.

Being there, what is it like?
    A chaotic, greedy, sexual child
            or

A wellspring of desire, love, and aggrandizement
> or

A fearsome place controlling or lacking compassion
> or

A cloudy fusion of body, mind, and soul
> or

A fantasy world of the collective unconscious
> or

A place of unity and peace
> or

A place unexplored of both darkness and light
> or

A cutting tool of constant enlightenment, a flimsy snow crystal,
my favorite enticement
> or

All of the above.

Being there, what is it like?

A chaotic, greedy, sexual child

From the toil and art of Freud, Adler, and Jung;
An engine of primitive energy and power
Transforms the sweet of all life's hope to sour;
A vacuum sucking air from the humanist's lung.

A monster uncontrollable, immutable, and punishing,
It mauled the ancient-born and much-nurtured hope,
Leaving its devoted and honest practitioners
Bereft of their faithful workhorse, rationalizing.

Being there, what is it like?

A wellspring of desire, love, and aggrandizement

Gushing from endocrine organs, hypothalamus, and
hormones
Entwined within an intricate anatomical structure.
Life and growth of feeling possesses our conjecture,

Producing undeniable, mind-displacing, sensual moans.

It is at that instant all that there could be.
It is at that instant all that could be desired.
It is at that instant all that might be imagined.
It is at that instant all that there is.
Poof, it is gone in a moment of passion, then satiation,
A spent feeling lost to memory, except for random procreation.

Being there, what is it like?

A fearsome place controlling or lacking compassion

Springing from all the cruel, self-absorbed power.
It slams into all social and familial strictures.
It lurks beneath a veneer of polite potentials,
Disrupted by intoxicants and often-tragic cerebral error.

Family, culture, society, and religion are standing guards
Against its raw, ruthless, domineering power.
These rationales are but a weak, crumbling barrier,
A faint firelight against dark, bumptious, barbaric hordes.

Being there, what is it like?

A cloudy fusion of body, mind, and soul.

The scattered clouds of an azure sky
Are punctuated by gray cumulus,
Fluming an aspiring mixture of incarnating, returning life
So ethereal, so beauteous, it draws a silent, serious sigh.

From smell of earth, toughness of rock, and sear of fire,
The aqueous but lowly, frail body sends vapors toward space.
They meet in sensual embrace, the changeable winds of mind,
Producing the precipitation of hot and cold, the soul's lyre.

Eureka and voilà, palpable, eternal inspiring music of spheres!

Being there, what is it like?

A fantasy world of the collective unconscious

Arising from the primordial mother sea,
Shocked by the first pulse of light,
Created by randomized accidents.
It is the product of light's electricity.

Throughout the eons of time,
It moved from molecule to cell,
From cell to groups of colony,
The froth of sensuous slime.

As the evolving race
Blossomed into unpronounceable species
From hard exoskeleton to stiff endoskeleton,
From brain to mind at a swift pace,
There formed the cellular precipitated phantom
Of ideas firmly embedded in the neural net,
Which sometimes trap us in a finite structure,
Except for a certain whim, an unevolved will, equally innate.

Being there, what is it like?

A place of unity and peace

Always at our volitional beck and call
Is the quietly beckoning light of insight,
The deep well of the inevitable silence inside,
The warm, firm love meditation can give us all.

It is there in sickness and health,
Like a true and loving marriage,
And it will last if we will it so
To our transforming end, our death
Marching through wealth and victory,
Steadfast companion in decline and failure,
A deep and splendid well, our resource

Turning inward, our personal congruency.

Always there,
But at a price
Of loving introspection,
There is meditation.

Being there, what is it like?

A place unexplored, of both darkness and light.

It is a place we have rarely gone,
A mysterious land with strange shapes
And sensations that play recorded tapes,
Reminding us of that which is long gone.

But as we know it not,
It is but a potential and unknown longing,
A thing that could enlighten
Or plunge us into blackness.
That could be our lot.

In spongy and willowy life and wisdom,
A spiritual and psychic space
That we can visit only by ourselves.
It is a surprising, unknown kingdom.
A plastic locus played on by the flashes of light,
A vast unchained universe of exploration
In which each particle possesses the all.
A beckoning journey of unknown duration
Without an inkling in our reality in time or our direct sight.

Being there, what is it like?

A cutting tool of constant enlightenment, a flimsy snow crystal.

There it awaits our approaching delight,
A gossamer device of intricacy
And subtle-shaping power,
A great gift of beauty: intrapersonal insight.

Like all tools of life and death,
It must be well used and loved
So it becomes what it was for.

That is
        To shape us to our best,
        To align us with the universe divine,
        To enable us with the power of love,
        To generate our potency to change.
So we must
        Choose our own contingencies,
        Be only what we will,
        Garner meaning from the all,
        Center it into our particular.

Being there, what is it like?
You cannot tell me.
I cannot tell you.
You cannot show me.
I cannot show you.
From only yourself, exercising a firmly seized freedom,
Can you learn what it is like
    For you now,
    For you then,
    For you tomorrow,
    And for your morrow.
What a gold mine of being and becoming!
What a human palatial construct!

Available for a lifetime,
We need little or no instruction,
It is
    Personalized
    Unique
    Chosen
    Changeable
    Evolving
    Fragile.
It is drawn from slowly energizing, empowering, and silent meditation.

Reflections on "Wherefore, in, of, and from Are You, My Unconscious?"

The concept of the unconscious has substantially transformed literature, history, philosophy, and even politics, but particularly the day-to-day experience of every person. It is astounding that the unconscious's past and current theoretical formulations were so vaguely attached to a database and its understanding so ill formed and, admittedly, bewilderingly occult.

In this poem, I move from the intensely personal to an abstraction. I will step onto what I believe to be new ground. I am grateful that no one can require me to have a reproducible and valid database to make these assertions. In this reflection, I hope to paint in broad strokes the principal theoretical underpinnings of this poem. They touch on Greek mythology, spiritual themes, and modern developmental and personality psychology as well as contemporary neurophysiology.

Early religions hint at the existence of a personalized unconscious. I know little about the specifics of religions, but I do have some acquaintance with Greek mythology. The gods acted as though people were of little consequence except when those filled with hubris affronted or disregarded them. The gods then took the mortals in rough and vindictive hands. They more often than not sealed the fate of a hapless mortal by transforming him into a flower—surely a boring but beautiful existence—as happened to Narcissus, who spurned the love of the nymph, Echo; or by torturing him endlessly, as happened to Prometheus, who, for stealing fire, was chained to a rock and whose liver was pecked eternally to a gory mess by a bird of prey. The gods inflicted pointed fates that were apparently derived from the deepest and most enduring personality traits of their victims. These traits, even weaknesses, were, in the case of Narcissus, self-love and, in the case of Prometheus, hubris and thoughtless rebellion or hostility toward the power of the gods. The timing of the gods' beneficence or victimization seemed whimsical. The gods themselves were all-powerful, or practically so, compared to our frail capacity to resist. This parallels the earliest psychiatric concepts of the unconscious as a driving and dynamic force that acts with irresistible power, with whimsy, and with consistency within the constraints of the person's personality and background. The gods' acts, paralleling this concept of the unconscious, also brought forth the pain or tragedy inherent in a given person's orientation to life, or weltanschauung.

The discovery and practice of hypnosis, medically investigated by Charcot, had a profound influence on Sigmund Freud. After attending Charcot's clinics and lectures, Freud developed a method to expose unconscious motivation underlying behavior. His work focused on those behaviors that were clearly contrary to the expressed intent of the person. Freud's powerful writing on humor and slips melded a stunning literary talent with a major discovery that, at first, created a firestorm in medicine, religion, and child development theory and then instigated a major change in medicine and in popular culture. His view was that the unconscious—the seething, power-hungry, asocial, tantrum-driven, polymorphous perverse, and sensual id—tainted and distorted the conscience to produce unintended behavior. Due to the love, the nurturance, and the ever-vigilant discipline of parents, combined with the child's deeply buried fear of the ever-present threat of a parent turning vindictive, vengeful, or even violent, the child's thoughts, feelings, and acts became a reasonable facsimile of a socially acceptable and productive lifestyle. Always lurking beneath superficially benign behavior were dark, driven, and powerful urges barely checked and molded by societal forces. This lifelong dynamic dictated a painful, endless war between darkness and light, in which only skirmishes were won. That war went on and on with little prospect of basking in a relaxed joy in the present and without any firm conviction of joy in the future.

The rebellion against this literary and culture-driven view of psychodynamics came first in the form of Watson's behaviorism. This was a weak, narrow, laboratory-based theory. It tried to explain learning and behavior as a mechanistic process. This theory largely ignored feelings and thoughts. It nevertheless widened the considerable cracks in the armor of psychoanalytic theory. Into these cracks, there came a movement based on a largely scientifically unverifiable theory called third force psychology (the first force was psychoanalysis; the second, behaviorism). The ideas of third force psychology, embodied in the work of Carl Rogers and more academically and powerfully by Abraham Maslow, resonated with all who view their life as an ongoing expression of intuition, dreams, and unanticipated inspiration. The concepts of Maslow's peak experience and of actualization offered an appealing perspective of yet another type of unconscious: an unconscious packed with altruism, wonder, awe, and gratitude. Unfortunately, this form of the unconscious lies dormant in most of us except for a lucky few who enjoy special brief moments of lucidity. The peak experience, stemming from the unconscious potential of all of us, suffuses the fortunate with boundless joy and the certainty of great power. These theoretical formulations suggest yet another concept of the unconscious that holds hope of empowerment, that needs only a release from unawareness, and that offers perhaps a too optimistic view of our potential. It is a concept that seduces me into a fond glow of love for mankind but requires a hard-to-sustain, pervasive suspension of skepticism.

It is my view that religion and particularly mysticism provide an enlightening perspective on the unconscious. Prayer, trance states, and meditation merge us with our environment, engendering a state that encompasses feeling as well as thought, in which we join the universe and the rest of mankind in true intimacy and abiding love. The most dramatic examples are the ascetic living alone in simplicity and apparent social deprivation and the whirling dervish or the Hasidic Jews transported during dances. However, meditation as practiced by millions brings to our awareness not only our bodily sensation but also our need for a fusion with the world. It is more a feeling than a thought, and one not entirely encompassed by the five senses or cognition. This new awareness, which seems an endless road of adventure and self-understanding, works almost imperceptibly into our daily life. It is, I suppose, part of the hardwired circuitry of our brain, a capability we all possess and a potential wealth we could all enjoy.

Jung postulated an archetypal brain based on the millions of years of evolution. The behavioral studies of animals in the wild show glimpses of the early development of this capability. Birds that have lived in total isolation nevertheless sing their genus-specific songs but without the specific local variations on the theme. Monkeys brought up without ever seeing a snake flee snakes in obvious terror. These behaviors must be hardwired in our brains: a genetic endowment expressed in behavior. If this is true for many animals, then must not the thoughts and feelings associated with the unconscious also be hardwired in human beings?

Konrad Lorenz's *Gedanken* (thought) experiment is one of the best examples. It points to a moral or humanistic component to the unconscious. You fantasize that you are sitting in front of a chopping board with a butcher's cleaver firmly in hand. First you take a head of cabbage and vigorously chop it up. Examine the feelings that this act engenders. Then you grab a grasshopper; you chop it up. How do you feel? Then a mouse, after that an infant monkey, and finally a human baby. Filled with horror by this fantasy, most people cannot finish the experiment even though it is mere fantasy. It is obvious that contemporary humankind, through political indoctrination and social coercion, has overcome this basic humanistic reluctance to be violent to other humans. Be thankful it is very difficult to completely wipe out this inborn pattern of kind and gentle feeling and thought toward those like us. We abhor brutality. During the Korean War, something like 50 percent of the American soldiers deliberately aimed their weapons above their targets. On deliberating on the meaning of this *Gedanken* experiment and how difficult it is to instill sufficient motivation in people to induce them to kill, I have found new meaning in the famous quote ascribed to Albert Einstein: "Imagination is more important than knowledge." Even though we are now capable of crunching numbers to an ever-increasing extent at ever-decreasing fractions of a nanosecond, perhaps our advance into a more humanistic future lies in our individual travels into the depths of the unconscious. After all, the unconscious is capable of melding feeling to thought, yielding life-giving wisdom rather than technical knowledge.

Steady, Quiet, Small Voice

In all of us, there exists a steady, quiet, small voice.
It is for us a choice.
Knowing it as steady, you learn your direction to the North Star.
It is your spiritual par.
Knowing it as quiet, you must listen always and always carefully,
As the world yells so stridently.
Knowing it as small, you will want to study it: to possess its feel
As your body's righting keel.

In all of us, there exists a steady, quiet, small voice.
It is for us a choice.

Yet so many there are in chaos benighted,
Who learned their direction from a world outside,
The love of their own voice never requited!
Having no inkling what they missed from inside,
Their compass arrow whirls
From the riptide of dreams of those they love
Or, much worse, from those with political power always errant.
These forces tangle their own dreams of their future.
Life's only treasure trove.

Knowing it as steady, you learn your direction to the North Star.
It is your spiritual par.

As the world on its axis wobbles,
Magnetic north shifts in a stable arc.
Based upon the iron core of our own world's oblate spheres,
So it must move with the times, the rhymes—simply, a lark

Of blossoming, mutating, growing, learning life.
Correcting its direction, not moved by whimsy and flashes
Riding over its sharp and rapid, irregular strife,

Corrected by reaction too hard to discern verities.
It closes in on life's asymptotic curve,
Always inaccurate but close enough to serve.

Knowing it as quiet, you must listen always and always carefully,
As the world yells so stridently.

The fanfare and frenzy of the world's demands drown our voice out,
But never entirely silences it.
We are charged to surround ourselves with survival without doubt,
Life can't always coexist with it.
If there's no room for both, there's nothing for it.
Life flees, while the result of its voice's action
Truly moves to outlive our inexorable death.
It grants an eternal presence, a finite creation,
The vibrant voice's ethos and process, life's lovely wreath.

Knowing it as small, you will want to study it: to possess its feel
As your body's righting keel.

Guiding you softly and lightly,
It moves toward a straighter line.
Being so, it corrects awareness slightly.
It is but a leaf-hidden but posted sign.
To stay always with what we believe, withstanding pain with endurance,
To be courageous, bold, and straight, to hold to the consequences,
To bargain and flex with peace, to love mostly through kind nurturance,
To ensure an enhanced future—these are man's natural sequences.

The steady, quiet, small voice within. One heeds. Obeys.
The consequence is man's release, his one true career.
We join the choral anthem from all the gods' voices,
The enchanting, winging, and soaring music of our expanding sphere.

Reflections on "Steady, Quiet, Small Voice"

Most of us simply accept and endeavor to comply with the demands of our society. What distinguishes great men and women from the rest of us is the capacity to turn away from the insistent, often-rewarding requirements of the world outside. People like Madame Marie Curie, Albert Einstein, Heinrich Herman Koch, Ignaz Philipp Semmelweis, Martin Luther King Jr., Mahatma Gandhi, Rauol Wallenberg, Chiune Sukiyama, Mark Twain, and Albert Schweitzer looked inside to that which was intuitively and logically right for them. It is an individual and personal revelation of the truth that demands action and is an imperative for a spiritually integrated life, an essential for a good life.

Many people act on their small voice of knowledge as if it were inevitable and right. Time often stamps the word *false* to their belief. Many lives may be troubled by or destroyed by their society's conviction that they are fanatics, crackpots, crazies, or weirdos. Unfortunately, often they are just that. On the other hand, if they are exactly on the course of the world's future, their acts resonate with the world's state of being. They initiate waves of change that engulf the world. The change comes through the emerging conviction of others that a person's acts lead to truth. For example, Mahatma Gandhi's *satyagraha*, "holding on to truth," or opposing injustice with love. Those so convinced become a majority because of the resultant benefit to all.

In their personal lives, these world shakers and movers, whose acts so enlarge and make the world more kind and loving, would be the first to acknowledge that they, more often than not, have failed to live up to the standards of their small voice. Examples are Gandhi's treatment of his wife and Martin Luther King Jr.'s affairs. Nevertheless, their life courses are like that of a sailboat's. A sailboat's course is never true. Its course meanders due to the influences of tide, wind, and waves, and most importantly, the helmsman's misperceptions. He always compensates for the action of the elements. What distinguishes masterful individuals is that they can perceive their own personal error. They correct deviant behavior based on the guidance of their small voice rather than purely on the demands of the world of society, politics, religion, personal power, or self-interest.

The capacity for insight alone is not enough. You must have the courage to carry out the dictates of your inner voice, always understanding that it may wander off the world's course. I imagine that greatness requires that you must act with conviction on what you believe, knowing full well it may be wrong. What is important is that you currently believe your voice to be right. Like a helmsman, you must constantly be able to correct this perception both through internal work and from the feedback life so freely and sometimes abrasively provides. To be content, reasonably happy, and fairly effective while doing this, you must never lose hope, optimism, courage, and humility. The essential feature of this approach is engaging, if not always enthralling. Its success lies in never foregoing even the most meager elements of enlightened self-interest.

I Decide

Him I call Brahmin
Who is free of bondage
To human beings and nature.
The hero who has conquered the world.

—from the *Bhagavad-Gita*

We who lived in concentration camps can remember the men who walked through the huts comforting others, giving away their last piece of bread. They may have been few in number, but they offer sufficient proof that everything can be taken away from a man but one thing: the last of the human freedoms—to choose one's attitude in any given set of circumstances, to choose one's own way.

—from Victor Frankl, *Man's Search for Meaning*

A monk asked Master Haryo. "What is the way?" Haryo said, "An open eyed man falling into the well."

—from a Zen Koan

There are laws of man.
There are laws of nature.
We may bow to the former.
We may submit to the latter.

But the laws of man
Are faulty, being only human.
They grind the bad and sometimes the good.
A higher law says law by the right stood.
    We recognize this as the finest,
    The mind of man at its best.

The law of nature

Can smash our energetic flutter.
>Yet we can choose to step into any space.
>Yet we can choose to die with honor.
>Yet we can choose the good fight.
>Yet we can choose from the light.
>To promote with our all what's right!

I always choose.
It is I who choose
>not the law of puny and fallible man,
>not the statute of proud, ignoble government,
>not the force and gritty drill of wealth,
>not the persistent demand of desire.

It is I who decides and chooses.
It is I who wins and loses.
It is just I
>not my body,
>not my mind,
>not their laws.
But I am, from my spirit alone,
Right or wrong, for or against everything.

Reflections on "I Decide"

I have always found it too easy to forget: I make every decision. I turn my face away from this awful truth. In the hurly-burly of my daily happenings, forces swirl about me like a dusty wind. "Do this," she says, while elongating the *this* with smiles full of promises. "Don't do that!" he says with the certainty of authority inversely proportional to the rationality or kindness of the command. "We are all going to," they say, as the crowd, laughing and talking, jostles along a smooth and downhill path. "You can't do that, or else I'll . . ." backed by the capacity to punish, delay, or derail you, your family, or even humankind. "After all," I remind myself, "he was right before" or "She did this for me, the least I can do is . . ." or "My God, how delicious that felt last time I did it!" My ego slips into the enticing matrix of someone else's will. Sometimes I am not even aware of whose will is being exercised. I lose my boundaries. Coercion gains power in the laxity of my mind. It bends to something outside my current ken.

I need to remind myself over and over. I need not do what seems the easiest, most acceptable, most rational. I need not even follow the laws of nature. I can choose to act according to my own judgment. By doing so, I infuse everything I do with a meaning defined by my act. What others think is not relevant unless I choose to see it as so. I can create meaning by being irrational, crazy, arbitrary, whimsical, absentminded, inconsiderate—by doing whatever I choose.

I surround myself with a translucent magic capsule. It is magical in that the outside world sticks to the capsule. I can reach from within and take whatever is on my capsule inside to become part of me. Whatever anyone says, whatever anyone does, whatever anyone feels or thinks—all this is projected onto my capsule. A small part of what is flying about sticks to the surface of my capsule. I sit within like a yoke in an egg. I must exercise my will to connect with what is on the outside of the capsule. I can examine it minutely on the capsule's wall before I take it in. Then I can deliberately decide to take all or only a part of what is on the wall inside to become part of me. I might try to take in only what is true.

This has consequences. What I take into the capsule becomes me. It melds with my personality. This is what my capsule will communicate to others within my sphere of influence. It is this process that shapes my life and continues to modulate who I am. A myriad of communications are sent. I take in a small part of them for my space within and for my future use in communicating to others. That will be who I am in the future. It is all a patchwork of melding and separating and me paring them down to what I can ingest. It is a rich life of deliberate give and take. What astonishes me is that the process works from inside out and outside in. How I love my kaleidoscopic in and out, my receiving and radiating though my capsule. How I will hate to give it up someday! How I hope I can give it up with joy when I vanish.

Only the Truth, a Mixed Blessing

My life, and all my private thoughts, are beset
With every genus and specie of regret,
For there are at least these two nagging voices
That speak to me of truth and its eternal choices.

These voices have not always been so loud or replete with clarity
To be a forced choice, an unavoidable necessity.
Too tough! I think. *That is a hard truth, certainly.*
Following these voices makes my life—unruly.

For my voices' commands are too exacting, too hard,
Or too demanding, too frustrating. A playing card
Dealt from life's deck, vicissitudes
Asking for Jesus-like attitudes.

All the love of and for children, so exhausting.
The pain of human flotsam so excruciating.
The tragedy of unlived lives full of grief, free of ecstasy.
The love of lives snuffed by the very nature of nature's law:
     whimsy.

I have a modicum of control,

Achieving it extracts a toll.
In its ceaseless insistence, I can always rejoice
By ever focusing on that still, small, eternal voice:

"Know the truth. It will set you free."
By means of that which only I myself can see.
The command never names its fee:
Trial, tribulation, fear, and calumny
Are the things it exacts from me.
I barter for pride and integrity.

Reflections on "Only the Truth, a Mixed Blessing"

It has been both a blessing and a curse that my whole life has been full of regret. More a blessing than a curse because it created a habit of reflection on what I was, am, and will be. Oftentimes, what I was, am, and will be were strangely at odds. Moreover, more often than not, the future shocked, astonished, and surprised me. There has been an everlasting nagging commentary within me that demands to be heard. When I start to do what this commentary so recently has righteously insisted upon, I find myself remonstrating, "Wait a minute! Are you sure you want me to do this?"

I *am* incredulous at my own commentary. I am irritated; I talk turkey to myself, "You just got done insisting that this was the right, no, the only right way to proceed. Now you say what about this and what about that? Didn't you have compelling reasons for your position? Why do you change your opinion so much? After all, I did not want to do it that way before, but you convinced me you were in the right."

My thoughts now wheedle. "Well, I thought what I said before was compelling." There is a pause and my monologue—if it could take hallucinatory human shape—shrugs. "But have you really thought of this. I had to reconsider. I mulled it over.

Don't you think you should too?"

"Well," I whine with more annoyance, "you seemed so sure, and you talked me out of what I thought was right. Don't you think you should think things through before you insist you are right?"

"Really I did, but then I thought of this and that. Now I think . . ." My vacillating mind drones on.

I find it difficult to follow myself, because I'm overwhelmed by and engrossed with my exploding irritation with this bodiless, wheedling, bargaining, whining, manipulating, and sophist monologue. All I can feel and think about is my irritation, a petty feeling too often followed by petty behavior. All I want is to have done with it all. Then my thoughts bring out something that catches my attention. Despite myself, I begin to think that this new reflection is correct. Maybe I should be listening more carefully.

My reflections now focus on my self-interest. I ask myself, "Where are these thoughts coming from? What ax are they grinding?" Then I reflect. "What does that matter if they prove their point?" Some other small, insistent thought chimes in. "Look out! This is a point. No, a needlepoint of danger! Remember that these contradictory points all come from you! Don't you know they are looking out for number one! Are they the *truth*? Or is it just what you want to be the truth?"

Turning on this new set of reflections, like a turkey on a rotisserie, I ask, rhetorically, because I don't want to hear my answer, "What are you, the truth police? Just because I think it would be good for me—that is, make me rich, powerful, sexy, and handsome—it doesn't mean it is wrong. Now does it?" Although I can't see the embodied source of my thoughts, I am certain he must be rolling his eyes. Then my reflections say so softly, forcing me to pay close attention, "How often does what you want to be truth, hope with all your heart to be truth, demand to be truth—because it would somehow be unfair to you if it weren't—really turn out to be the truth?"

I know my questions refer to the truth that being right has not much, if anything at all, to do with what I want. It has to do with what *is*, even if it hurts. Oh, hell! I think my ongoing monologue—the little bastard—won't let me lie and *not know it*. Lying to myself would be so much easier if I did not know I was doing it. Knowing that I am lying will not set me free to soar to whatever place of truth is possible.

But what about those ankle weights that I have fashioned throughout my life? I fashioned them with the help of my friends; my parents; the forever-mistaken, hypocritical, power-hungry authorities; and life itself. No one is saying truth travel is easy, but the view en route is very special. It is definitely worth the trip, even with all its expense, hardship, and need for patience.

Have the Wit, Be Happy

Always a source of amusement,
If I laugh with myself.
Always a source of amusement,
If you laugh with yourself.

I will know what it was meant to mean
During my life-drawing inevitable twists.
You will know what it was meant to mean
During your life-drawing inevitable twists.

I talk as if life has its own way.
And that is exactly what I mean to say.
We are just so and made so as to declare
With every willful act, cosmos' intent we dare
To test, to understand the basic facts, to bare?
That is, all to uncover.
Our designer truths to endure.

Daunted by the intricacy of the physical world,
We embrace boldly what eludes
Any resemblance to the meaning of words.
Man, a silkworm, enclosed his own mystery
In a colorful cocoon of semantic structures.
They are only useful if attempting to find the worm of life's meaning:
Experiences, fantasies, thoughts, dreams,
Accidents, books, scenes, and pictures
Narrowly yet inevitably they have escaped us.
It is only the cabala of all our own striving.
Our fate is not to fathom the character of God.

That sour milk curdles is not a cosmic joke.

Disappointing, but merely natural law.
All peoples, without exception, heavens create;
I guess it is a major pastime of every bloke.
To use his wit to understand futility.
So let's laugh, enjoying its utility.

There is no other intelligent choice!
You may laugh with the rest of us.
If you have the wit, be happy.
Why not, though some dub you sappy?

Reflections on "Have the Wit, Be Happy"

We live oblivious to what is most humorous in our lives. We do not look at ourselves with the eyes of a child. More often than not we don't look at ourselves at all. Perhaps I generalize ascribing my own way of being to you.

In years past, I lived in troubled ignorance of who I was. To this day, it is an effort to see, hear, and feel, sense—what is it I do, what are *my* thoughts, and what are *my* feelings? I marvel at the wide and wonderful world. I have not attended sufficiently to myself. Everything outside of me looks more orderly, more effective, more interesting, more beautiful, and most importantly, less painful than seeing myself through the wise eyes of a child.

To see, hear, and feel what it is I do, what I think, and what I feel is like solving a puzzle that seems to be always just beyond my comprehension. When I attempt a puzzle or riddle or even try to help my eighth-grade son with an algebra word problem, I am overwhelmed with frustration. Ominous thoughts rush into my mind. My feelings swirl around the unfairness of the problem. Its unreasonableness in its demand on me. When I stay with this feeling, I unravel like a ball of yarn harried by a kitten. These troubling sensations vex me. I am certain they must be someone else's fault. When I stay with these thoughts, I am awash with hostility. How can I grab it? Why is it beyond me? Why should someone so lovable as I be teased and taunted in this way?

Struggling to achieve insight yields a realization that true understanding is always beyond our capability. A comedian can rip our sensibilities with foreseeable mistakes, which engender pity for his embarrassing ineptitude. Observing our mental processes focused on insight has a similar feeling tone. Our natures are more elaborate and quicker than our most focused and thoughtful intellectual insight can muster. We cannot simply step aside and just let ourselves be without seeking insight.

Freud dissected the mind and found what he was looking for in the unconscious. He found what he was looking for because there were so many universes in the mind available to explore. There were infinite transformations of who we are in bewildering varieties. He developed a technology, and ever since, we had been lured into exploring the mind. His method (psychoanalysis) is arguably the father of all therapies. It shared with its progeny a serious fault. It was vulnerable to nonrandom bias of personal rationalization or self-serving politicization as well as a huge amount of random error. The basic reason for its usefulness is that we have sculpted so many wonderful and bizarre views of the mind based on these theories. The unconscious is like carnival mirrors, where each mirror distorts both the shapes of and the colors of the mind and where each mirror also reflects thoughts, feelings, and behavior characterizing the mind of a given individual with different degrees of accuracy. What is so awe-inspiring is that many of these images yield substantial and useful truths.

You could say, "Well, perhaps mental health requires restraint in our need to comprehend, explain, and explore!" There is truth in that, but unfortunately, I think we have no choice. It seems to be our nature to strive to grasp our meaning, actually the meaning of God, if we were created in his image. We are always coming closer to our meaning. If we turn away from trying to understand our purpose and meaning, we are condemned to live a life of avoidance. We might as well say we can live without breathing or love without sexuality or agape or swim without moving through water. Our tragedy is that we know that to grasp the meaning of our lives is forever out of our reach.

The Shining Self

Our adversaries are without, within!
Setting aside our smaller circle dubbed sin,
Look to that wild dark kernel inside.
It is ever with corporeal life closely allied.

That immediate impulse to survive
Over principled goals yearns to override.
Pulsing hour by hour, draw back from animal desire.
The full shining self is the generative power.

From self-nurtured and voluntary power,
Steadfastly shining from our soul's tower,
A beacon! The shining self! Expands through all,
It is will-enabled, weighing against the world's pressure.

Will is a finer enlightening guidance
Than our darkness, which provides but a hindrance—
A pleasure-strewn path to dodge, a maze, an obstacle
To learning from the shining self, our certain oracle.
    By contesting our darkness,
    We are tending our lightness.

Reflections on "The Shining Self"

*I found in myself, and still find, an instinct toward a higher, or, as
it is named, spiritual life, as do most men, and another toward a
primitive rank and savage one, and I reverence them both.*
　　　　　　　　　—from *Walden* by Henry David Thoreau

The outside world penetrates our spirit's marrow. Yet we possess a
persistent stubbornness. It is a faint, often failing, but never defeated
conviction. There is a way to live what is the best, the brightest, the most
humane in our spirit.

The darker side of our internal life is demanding. I am not talking about
sin. I see sin as a cleverly and, perhaps deliberately, fashioned concept. Sin
was created and sold by humans to humans. Its purpose was to alienate and
bedevil humankind's natural inclinations. Rather, I mean the darkness inside
that works in concert with the demands of the world. It is a much broader
concept than sin. This darkness is our lusts, our passions, our naked need for
power. It enhances them by giving them an enticing and seductive veneer
of worthiness. It lurks within, struggling to join the immediate gratification
that the world offers so wantonly. It calls to be embraced. All one need do is
to overlook the insistent opposing demands of what one senses is humane,
powerful, and uplifting.

Yet everyone's darker side is a great teacher. It silhouettes the dangers
of an unconsidered, not chosen, or seemingly coerced life. Such a life—
being deprived of the enlightenment of the broadest self-interest—cannot be
impeccable and an expression of loving kindness.

Self-interest has a bad reputation. It is confused with greed, narcissism,
indifference, horrifying cruelty, and monomaniacal pursuit of personal goals.
I refer to a specie of self-interest based on the expression of the urges to

build, to unite, to expand, to render kindnesses, and to enable what is best in us to fruition. Yes, even to enjoy the orgasms of mind and body with complete abandon. Such a consciously chosen self-interest is the culmination of what is best in us. It is also what I have seen in my patients as I work with them in therapy. I firmly believe conscious self-interest leads to a steady progression toward a humane culture. We could make such a choice every minute of our lives. Why not?

SECTION III

WHAT'S OUT THERE?
FROM WITHOUT:
THEIR ATTACK

Crazy Coffee Poem or
A Therapist's Addiction

Oh, coffee, coffee! How I love thee!
You certainly suit me to a T.
As anyone can easily see,
Coffee engenders glee
    And helps his "therapee."

Coffee could be humanity's key
Were it not for seas of pee.
And were it not for fragrant coffee,
Very sleepy I would be
    And lost to "therapee."

Reflections on
"Crazy Coffee Poem"

What is enthralling and challenging to do occasionally—that is, to bond and understand at the same time—is another matter, if it must be sustained for eight or nine therapy hours a day. To do that for eight to ten clients per day is very demanding. Perhaps it cannot be done up to standard in an eight-hour day. In moderation, coffee helps, even though it leads to certain technical problems. That is where my tongue-in-cheek poem comes in.

What is a therapist to do to bond and understand? How does that help his client? Simply put, he must listen. Have you ever thought about those hours upon hours spent listening? The therapist cannot swill alcohol to allay his anxiety, cannot smoke to have something to do with his hands, cannot reminisce about his most recent, fascinating, and quirky bout of lovemaking, cannot fondly recall sinking a snake of a putt, cannot fume about how wrong and pigheaded his wife (or husband or lover) was in his last argument, cannot even focus on not letting a noisy fart go, and cannot worry about whether he paid the last electric bill or whether he has enough money to pay the taxes, mortgage, etc. He should not even be overly concerned about when the fifty-minute hour is over. He must focus on what is being said, how it is said, how it might feel to say it, or what is not being said and how that might feel. When he does it well, the patient senses this, is enchanted, and more importantly, empowered by it.

In the last analysis, a therapist is paid to listen for 90 percent of the time and to say something not far off the mark during the other 10 percent of the time. It does not even matter very much what he says as long as the therapist believes it is kind, true, and necessary. After that, of course, he must attempt to communicate to the patient that what he has just said or done was, in fact, an attempt characterized by kindness, truth, and necessity.

When a therapist says something in his precious 10 percent of the therapy hour devoted to what he opines, he modulates the relationship. Over time, his listening actively and empathetically has infused the relationship with meaning. This has given the relationship power. The meaning of the relationship impacts the balance of what goes on between therapist and client—that is, the stable fulcrum of the balance that changes both. If he hits the mark with his interpretation, observation, or commentary, what he says adds value of improved process and goals moving toward alignment with rational self-interest. If he misses the mark by an inept, inaccurate, or slightly off intervention, the value of the relationship forces the client to revise or rectify the therapist's intervention and to communicate the truth of the matter from his point of view. In short, he corrects the therapist, achieving the requisite and desirable insight. The net effect is the same from both an accurate or inaccurate intervention. It may be salutary if and only *if* the therapist's intervention bears the wholesome quality of truth, kindness, necessity, and in addition, is mounted with the client's well-being as the controlling and guiding factor.

While dealing with therapists, most patients take offense at two things: the therapist not saying enough or not listening. By far, the error that produces the most damage to the relationship is not listening. After all, most patients know that the therapist is beset and bewildered by many of the same problems the clients find so insurmountable. More often than not, the clients do not really believe the therapist does much better at coping with the same life problems as they do. They just hope he does and have sufficient skill to let them in on his secret. This conception or misconception justifies the money they are shelling out. In this regard, amazingly, hope does spring eternal. Am I saying something out of turn?

What the clients do not realize or very seriously doubt is that they have all the answers inside of themselves. They can formulate the questions as well as decide which must be borne and which could be changed by means of their own cognition and exercise of will. They even have the ability to plot how to make the changes as long as the therapist subtly provides them the power, the potency, and the permission to advance courageously to the trials and tribulations normally required to make any change. But this realization is like a hard and dirty job that stares the patient or client in the face and demands he take action or accept the consequences. It is so hard to get started and so overwhelming to face those conflicts in life that have no painless solutions. Such a job goes better when two work together. The therapist helps the patient stay on track and keeps his own frustrations, mistakes, and biases from being an obstacle. Make no bones about it, the therapist is working on those same conflicts and profoundly benefits from the insight of his patients. If the therapists cannot benefit from their clients' struggles, I hold they are not therapists in the profoundest and most professional sense of the word. Every one of our clients or patients is a teacher! Listening to them is not only the key to help them but also to learn about ourselves. And coffee? Well, coffee helps us to pay attention.

(I apologize for the male chauvinism indicated by the choice of *he* rather than *one* or *he and she*. I have used male pronouns to meld the reality of low bladder capacity of, especially aged, males to the meaning of the poem.)

Forgoing the Pot of Gold for Running the Rainbow

The tire flattened,
A gush of air.
It punctured my travels, thwarted my determination.
I stood idle and anxious outside my car.

Kind travelers paused and asked, "Could I help?"
Politely, I declined, waiting quietly
For the tow-truck driver.
I hoped for some help before light waned.

Rumbling up, a stuttering stop, squealing brakes.
The driver—tall, ugly, lean, and angular—steps out.
After a few inquiries, he takes
My keys to check the spare.

It was as flat as the flat, towing was the only out.
I berated myself for thoughtlessness and lack of care.
Impatient and disturbed, I saw him as a gibberish-spouting lout.
His derision swept past me like air from my blown tire.

We left with my car in tow. I dozed.

I woke to his drumming, *tit-tat-tit-tat-tat*.
At the light, his hands flashed, winging over the engine sound.
A sound strong, complex, and compelling so that I sat
Spellbound by his talented drumming drumsticks.

"How in the world did you learn to drum like that?"
"I work every night, most nights of the week,
Long hours of waiting or sleeping like a lost cat."
He sighed, "'Cause I always wanted to drum, I took lessons."

"Do you want to play with a band?"
I imagined his reply: "I just learn whatever—to move along.
Each week my teacher sets tasks to my hand,
And I become drumsticks by playing with what there is to learn.

"I started by looking for the pot of gold.
I lusted to pass through the sky, up and down the rainbow's arc,
To fly to some glistening goal, as some myth foretold,
To find what I could do and, by that end, exceed myself.
"The stars flashed by, streaks of light,
Scratched the sky,
Made by my flight
In swirling, sweeping arcs.

"My sticks danced, perfecting mind's ear in this grungy cab,
Bounded across the steering wheel,
Making this prison lively, making artful these daily events' drab.
Through my effort, my desire can be fulfilled.

"More than pots of gold found at rainbows' ends.
I was beginning, trip, end, all,
Becoming by learning, playing were what I will intend
To be devoured by striving, singing in my head!

"My need to learn, may it ever—never err,
To let my mind's ear see through my hands, beat the beat of the wheel,
Fly through the dark night air to ascend
The overarching arc onto great circle routes.

"I speed along the arc. I have taken a hold,
Moved along by my creative spirit
Moving beyond the pot of gold.
I ride the rainbow of heavenly sound."

So we came to the gas station,
Where he eased my car down,
Where the tire was inflated,
From where,
From now on,
I travel with spirit rhythm
To an inspiring destination.

Reflections on "Forgoing the Pot of Gold for Running the Rainbow"

My life has been full of accidents that spawn insights. I suppose I am not unique in this regard. Yet I must constantly remind myself that where I think I am going is not where I am headed. There is a paraphrase ascribed to Yogi Berra: "If you don't know where you are going, you will end up someplace else." "Running the rainbow" asserts the opposite: It is often good to end up someplace you did not know you were going. Chance can be the mother of spiritual invention. The driver of the tow truck did not say what I quote him to have said. I firmly believe that is what he meant to say, had the situation allowed him to say it. He could have communicated what I wrote. It only required me to be open to what was happening, leaving off trying to control my life, experiences, thoughts, and sensations. This benefit eludes most of us in our society, which puts a premium on efficiency and bringing home the bacon. Yet fixedly pursuing my planned aims is a roadblock to my understanding and enlightenment. Is it for you as well?

Often I am not open. I accomplish this by terminating conversations, by sticking to schedules, by being on time, by working enough to pay all my seemingly ever-increasing bills, and by looking for something new in everything I read. These are just a few of the ways I avoid what I could learn and experience. By terminating conversations, chance remarks or confidences are lost. By sticking to schedules, my mind cannot run free to explore fully what is at hand. By working enough to pay for everything I think I need, I cannot let life's unexpected events put wisdom in my grasp. By looking for something new in what I read, I fail to absorb fully and meld completely with what is already there that creates a new understanding. In short, I forget that it is the journey, not the destination, that births enlightenment.

We all have some gift. Our gifts are like the fragrance of flowers. A blossom does not decide or plan to smell good. To give, we need not decide to give. Our gifts are the by-product of what we do as humans, our very being. Flowers are us, in our largest and best sense. But to take in this gift, this by-product of being, we must give up something. We must focus on what is happening as opposed to what we want to happen. We must loosen the constraints of our day-to-day assembly-line reality to appreciate the accidents of communication from the world around us. That way we take in fearlessly the heavenly fragrance from earthbound flowering.

To See the Diamond Stars in the Sky

For age is opportunity no less
Than youth, though in another dress.
And as the evening twilight fades away
The sky is filled with stars, invisible by day.

—Henry Wadsworth Longfellow

So we move upwards
As we lose our hold on
Things we have wrestled with forever.
In the rush of disappearing youth,
We join the experiences of the aged.

Sense of attachment
Becomes detachment.
We fade away through
    Loss of prowess,
    Weakening orgasms,
    Faltering senses,
    Foreclosed futures,
    Growing wisdom.
In our changing world,
Aging never changes.

We fall behind in the column of life.
Younger, lighter feet tramp on and on.
And we, deluded by youthful truths, errors, hopes,
Wander, wonder, awake and aware.

With love, we are left alone like an old Eskimo.

We are consumed by a dwindling fire.
Physical presence is disbursed in starry dust,
Leaving traces in ever-changing worlds—
Scattering curves in hyperspace.
Our diminishing life sheds a spirit eternal.

Whatever that may be,
It is always our choice,
Shaped through intention and process.
Goals are often missed.
We could wed intention and process
    To kindness,
    To respect,
    To agape,
Never give up these goals.
That is what we can do in life:
What a magnificent endeavor!
A privilege to live, love, create, and die.
My friend, fix your eye on diamonds in the sky.

Reflections on
"To See the Diamond Stars in the Sky"

There is both an algebraic and physical-chemical function to life. Of course, death is part of life, the end surely, nevertheless an integral part. At birth, we are not capable of much, physically or mentally, except an almost boundless capacity to charm parents through gurgles, burps, gas smiles, poops, wandering gaze, and random jerky movements. We orchestrate our lives, announcing "We are here." We are a heartwarming sight: chubby, dimpled, soft, helpless, and vaguely resembling our proud and beaming parents. We are mostly potential. Endowed with a basic hardwired and genetic potential, we are a slate with borders. Parents can write anything on the slate, but the borders limit them. We can write anything that has both intrigued and bedeviled us. We can write cruelty through indifference. We can write focused hatred. We can write boundless self-absorption. We can write arrogance and pride. We can write courage, nobility, and overarching agape, not limited to the human species but including all life. We are writing our life book out of necessity, as our very survival depends on it. Without courage, nobility, and agape, due to our seeming boundless potential for inducing catastrophe, we are surely doomed to nuclear holocaust or perpetual, episodic lemminglike genocides.

As parents, the first writers on the infant's slate, most of us understand that writing courage, nobility, and agape is the only course likely to sustain our cultural evolution and maintain our survival. Looking back on history, it is astonishing how long it took us to realize that we are one. What is good for me is good for you. I am thankful to live in an age where perceiving ourselves as one looms ever larger and more certain in the world's culture.

At first it is the parents who write on the slate and learn to live with its limitations. As the infant grows to babyhood, the parents begin to guide the hand of the toddler in writing on its slate. As the child proceeds to adulthood, the parents' power diminishes. Our potency to dictate the course of our children's lives is reduced eventually to impotence. Or heaven forbid, we must influence the course of our child's life by example and through love bonded to enlightened self-interest. From toddlerhood through young adulthood, a child grows stronger and seizes control of its own writing. The growing child can overpower the influence of the parents. The parents never accept impotence in trying to edit their children's slate. They become less a parent but remain a major but sometimes unwanted contributor to the slate, either through excessive compliance, hostile opposition, or various types of unconscious but subtle guidance. Parents can become collaborators, giving and receiving, teaching and learning, as loving adult companions or friends to their grown children.

It is hard for most of us to accept that we become the true and only authors of our life's slate. We ourselves do the final editing. This realization grows as we age and becomes ever more apparent as we begin to notice our own loss of power, pleasure, and potency. We struggle to maintain control and soon learn that while we entirely control our process, the goals are astonishingly and inevitably elusive. What is the actual goal achieved is often not intended. Our goals squirm away, producing effects that are often unpredictable, frequently whimsical, and sometimes costly or even tragic. We can no longer point to Father or Mother or even their belated surrogates (authority figures) as the author of our life events. We cannot blame their ripple impact on those we love or hate. We can and should—oh, there is that awful word—write on our slate only what we want to give to the world.

During this process, we shift away from personal power to being overwhelmed by the world's power. As our bodily prowess wanes, the impact we have created changes the nature and quality of the universe. In the last few centuries, man's capacity to change the universe has increased through advances in technology. Eventually we die. We become elements dispersed among the stars. However, what we have done and how we did it lives on in some form forever. Our ripple effect on the universe is endless. We must never loose sight of our impact. While the intended impact differs from the actual impact, it is the degree of courage, nobility, and agape characterizing our process that makes our lives worthwhile. Eventually we die. Let us go with our eyes steadfast on the stars.

Horizons Only Confine You

Early on, in my sloop, *Seafair*, sailing,
I learned of a balm for seasickness.
"Look well beyond the swells
To the receding horizon,
    And surely you will feel better."

Alone, I walked on the beach.
Sandpipers stepped in the water's wash.
Seagulls squalled of endless need;
Pelicans' wings caressed swelling surf.
    And I did feel better.

Going beyond birds in feathered flight,
I was enthralled by the warring waves,
Curling crests clawing in,
Driving sandpipers back and forth.
    And to me, the world felt better.

Beyond the oily smooth breakers,
Wind driven from far sea expanse,
Caressed, misting the sky,
Fogged finely with spray and foam.
    This spot in the cosmos became me.

Then I wondered what was still beyond.

Eye of mind clearly sculpted visions,
Without structure, without firm form.
Things beyond our horizon,
    Their grandeur fills my fantasy.

When at sea and yawing of your mind
Gives rise to disabling nausea,
Look beyond horizons!
Center your mind's vision!
    And you will be—simply spellbound.

When life's paths shut you down,
Threatening a painful darkness,
Trash your tight circle.
See spray-loaned spirit sans form.
    You know what is beyond yourself.

Move to what you could become.
Fire your joy through being out there.

Reflections on
"Horizons Only Confine You."

One night, when my children were young, far from the lights of the city in the mountains of the High Sierras, I woke from cold. Looking around me, I was disoriented and frightened. The spilled frost of the Milky Way lay within the boundaries of the small black and perfectly flat lake. No wind disturbed its mirrored image. I turned my head to the moonless sky to see the Milky Way populated by a hundred billion stars. Focusing on the stars on a dark night, though each was so small, it seemed we might scoop them up with a cupped hand. Their majesty dwarfs mankind, so many have said. I recalled that strontium from the stars lies quietly in everyone's bones. Truly, we are what the stars are made of. As I zipped my sleeping bag so as to be warmed, I felt a grandeur that warmed my spirit. Fear vanished without startling me. The vastness and beauty of the cosmos did not diminish me. How could it since I am that vastness?

It is a medical maxim that looking at the horizon helps to diminish the nausea of seasickness. It reestablishes one's balance by diminishing the apparent motion of the boat. Such a simple act of will in the face of a rising gorge improves homeostatic equilibrium and calms the neurophysiological events in the semicircular canals, the saccule, and in the nuclear centers of the medulla oblongata and midbrain. These are the complex functions in humans that provide the database for all progress through space. Similar systems operate in all creatures that locomote. Parallel systems, no less basic, must operate to locomote amongst the largely uncharted networks of mind and spirit.

There is no real hierarchy. These centers deep within the brain are an integral part of our highest functions. If you do not believe me, just ask someone unfortunate enough to suffer from vertigo. Yet every disability, short of death or severe brain damage, may be overcome by willing its subordination to functions of the most highly developed part of us. These are cognitive functions, our true masters and, also, loyal slaves. Others might call it our spirit. I am speaking of what remains after discounting our feelings, thoughts, and acts. Yet it is always a stretch for us. Much of literature and philosophy seems to be only a thinly veiled complaint against what is seen as a surrender to our animalistic nature. I would contend that there is no real or substantial separation or difference between our baser functions and our highest, except what can be measured as the application of will to become and be. Truly, we reach for the stars, when not overwhelmed and bedeviled by our immediate needs. But how far must we reach when they are within every one of us? They are our very essence, as they always seek a naturalistic expression when we give them half a chance to fly.

The Enchanted Dream

A parable redrawn:

> A Chinese philosopher, perhaps Lao Tse, was talking to a king. The king told him that he had fallen into a deep sleep. He had dreamed he was a beautiful butterfly. He awoke from his dream and felt sad that he was no longer a butterfly flying from flower to flower in an enchanted world. The philosopher commented by asking him, "How do you know you are a man dreaming of being a butterfly? Could you not be a butterfly dreaming he was a man?" The king found this concept of life so intriguing that he believed himself to be an enchanted butterfly dreaming he was a man for the rest of his life.

What can we have in life?
Maybe we can have one thing we want?
We certainly can't have everything we might want.
Often that one thing comes from immense strife.

Or maybe we could be one of those rare butterflies
Gifted, so gifted with lustrous beauty or supersonic flight,
Someone like Gandhi, Einstein, Madame Curie, or Mozart
Who soars on a honed mystical mentation, then dies.
Yes, that is right, dies likes the rest of us,
Who all enter into the realm of what is not being
For all time. But everyone has had their say about
The where, the what, the why, the who
That was the life they created.

There are those who are certain about what it is like.

Then there are those who know one cannot be certain.
They choose to refrain from saying what it could be,
Like me, 'til the lightings of an enchanted dream strike.

Last night my long-dead, beloved dog defended me against a sharp-toothed hyena.
In the dark of night, I roamed London in a lush garden decorated by a wooden bear.
That was during the intermission from a musical based on a Dickens's story
Using familiar Beetles' melodies played though a smoky glass enclosure.
Music wrapped my ears as I wandered in the audience scattered about,
Characters from a life I could have had, had I not chosen the one I choose.
Given a lift by a kind London trio, I lied that I met the Princess of Wales.

Yes, that's right, dies like the rest of us.
If I could mandate the afterlife, then
No harps with soporific music of the spheres for me.
No benign light cast against gliding shadows for me.
No infinitely complex nexus of understanding for me.
No everlasting, never "too intense" orgasm for me.
No being awash with the sensations of life for me.
No dark and abysmal absence of everything dear for me.

Instead, the kaleidoscope of enchanted dreams
    Without the constraints of reality!
Of what could have been had I chosen amongst
    All the other possibilities of life,
Had I not chosen the life I did in fact choose
    Quite well, despite ever-present regrets.

Reflections on "The Enchanted Dream"

Most of us get to choose a life. I chose a life with a dreamlike quality. I am always deeply enmeshed, yet I never really understand any part of it. My multiple understandings of my dreams confront and confuse me. I can never see all of them at once. If I did, it would always be changing, some sleight of hand, a joke on reality. We want to believe a dream has one more or less accurate meaning. Consider the possibility that all interpretations of our dreams are true, though mutually contradictory. After all, are we not a complicated and finely fitted art piece?

Sometimes I am enthralled just to come close to a practical comprehension of my dream and therefore my life. For dreams to be so incomplete and shifting may seem painful to you. I do not experience it that way. It is an essential part of life's joy for me. There is always the hope that the current comprehension may lead to a spiritual and physical fulfillment beyond past pleasures however physically orgiastic or intellectually exciting they may have been. Perhaps that's realizing life is there whether I am alive and in it or not. We have an opportunity to partake but know it is not forever. Not only will it be taken away by time through aging and then dying but also through satiation. And the lust for the dream life trails off, only to be born anew. That is always a wonder to me: that each moment passes only to be surpassed by another of enthrallment. Would heaven be this state, a multimirrored image of the life we lead, or some other abstract of our dream life? But our state is frozen into a certain history by the sweeping hand of the clock.

It Is Out There, Isn't It?

I think it is out there.
Isn't it?

I am Elsa, the Nobel laureate of snow macaques,
The discoverer of swimming and salting potatoes.
And look, many of those males step over the novel toys on our paths.
Not me!
On to something new, different, and better.
They do not believe! I do!

I founded mankind,
Then I left Africa to populate the world.

I was the first farmer,
Then I left my plants and place.

I left home, family, friends
To practice freely the one true religion in the New World.

I climbed Everest.
"It was there."

I believed love is stronger than force.
India became free to make its own mistakes.

I will leave the running waters and green trees
For the disconcerting spin of the titanium space station,
One short stopover on my way to a planet's paired and burdened star.

Then the cosmos.

When I get to its expanse and geometrically tricky border,
What then?
Then where will I go with purpose but with false belief?
Dismaying thought. No?

Why am I so sure about what I believe
When there is nothing to base my belief on?
So I believe Muhammad without foundation—
Or rather, no more foundation than believing in Christ
Or Moses or Buddha or Oral Roberts or Adolph Hitler.
Baseless beliefs are held close, even unto death,
When beliefs with factual basis are struggled with and altered,
And never blindly loved but affectionately examined and tightly held.

Is the reason for these false and fixed beliefs
To free me to move away from what is known
With conviction
To what is not known, claiming that it is better?
Without absolute certitude?
Could we do anything different now,
If we were not certain
That what we are now doing is somehow
Less than what we expect to be doing in the far-reaching and grand future?

Believing that something else is better, different, or especially fascinating—
That delusion drives us into the unknown, thinking it can be known.

Reflections on
"It Is Out There, Isn't It?"

Is it not astonishing that some people leave what is known for what is unknown? Sometimes they flee what is overwhelming them, feeling that staying has nothing but personal disaster to offer. This motive for doing something different is not admired; it is coerced. But some people move outside the reach of what they know and have dealt with dislocation for years, more or less successfully for a different, less rational reason. They want to do something where the outcome is unknown but potentially grand and idealistic. The brain yearns for novelty, the vitamin of the intellect. The process of these life changes promises only hardship, failure, discouragement, exhaustion, and sometimes, even death. The curious, the restless, the hunters, the pioneers expend fortunes, immense amounts of energy, sometimes most of their lives, and the good will and companionship of friends and relatives, all to achieve something, the very nature of which is unknown or barely imaginable—from riding an unicycle across a continent to climbing the highest mountain without companions or oxygen. Or from allowing their fingernails to grow for a lifetime until they are yards in length, to traveling to Mars. Or from rowing in an open boat across the Atlantic Ocean to detailing the theory of relativity or superstring theory. Why? On the face of it, such acts are certainly insane. Could it be that this insanity is a part of the essence of humankind?

This desire for something unknown, perhaps unknowable, and almost certainly less comfortable than what one already has characterizes what we think of as best in ourselves. The need to do these things overwhelms reservations of rationality and practicality. It is universally admired by the vast majority of people who might exclaim, "Me? Not on your life," then ruefully, "But he did it. Fascinating and wonderful. I like that." Not all of us possess that desire, but even some animals have it.

And now we are about to launch into space, a daunting, uncertain, and vastly expensive venture. We certainly have not mastered all the problems we have right here on Earth. We seem doomed to carry those earthly problems into the cosmos, infecting everything with our cultural malaise. Eventually we will run out of room. What then? But think of this. Maybe there is more than one cosmos or perhaps even many anticosmoses. Or if not, we may be forced to return to our already-occupied space. Then we will be forced to deal with what we have not yet accomplished here in order to achieve the unknown. Anyway, this eventuality is far into the future. You and I will not be here. We will not have to deal with it. So I guess it is safe to assume that we will, for all practical purposes, never be forced to solve our current problems, especially our psychic ones, as we are too busy spreading them. This is a delusional cultural system of magnitude and depth, a cosmic psychosis. There is no magic pill for this psychosis. Perhaps it is not an illness. It might be part of our health. Be it a mental illness or not, we secretly enjoy and thrive on our delusional system. Ultimately, it may well be part of out DNA. The unknown is the epigenetic factor (an environmental factor that is a prerequisite to the expression of a gene) that gives the gene expression in our behavior.

A Trail of Dried Tears

From the edges of both his eyes, I could see a trail of dried tears.
—from an investigative report of a child-abuse
case resulting in death.

We all suffer,
But there are those special children
Who encounter the obscene rage of whippers,
Who try to muffle their whimpers.

What comes to hand
Slashes the flesh of innocents—
Belt or buckle, clothes hanger, or board.
Lord, lay it on . . . Laid on raised blood tears, Oh Lord.

Has he turned
His face away from that child
Who does not know a firm hand granting caresses?
Who aches without hope for all those soothing kisses?

Smooth all their brows.
Build sanctuary in self-image.
It is only love that soothes most cares,
Smooching away telltale salty trails of dried tears.

A child is harshly spanked
By a mother who loves.
This act reveals the need lives within the spanker.
Faulty love defeats misguided cruelty.

The child who knows love will grow
Strong, true, surviving pain;
Though beaten, he thrives on love and concern.
From parents and us he will not turn.

But fear that child!
Love free, fed whimsical pain.
He becomes a predator; he flashes anger's fire.
We shun him in disgust and fear. Justice we require.

Savoring anger,
Angry blows bred, free of concern;
He yearns to throw savage pitches,
Flashing on, off, on . . . like manic light switches!

Without empathy's employ,
He will wound and destroy
Both our lives—their safety and joy.
Dealing us destruction, grief, and enduring angers,
We persecute him
Whose abuse left dried, unkissed, untended tears.

Could we choose to do otherwise?

We lock him in a dark isolation!
Alone to roil in his hostility!
Without sympathy or comprehension,
We cauterize with electricity.
We resolve not to heal our grief born of loss and catastrophe.
With anger, we fail him by withholding compassion for his tragedy.

Could we choose to do otherwise?

Alloyed with oh so many family ties,
Victims' and victimizers' tragedy buys
Painful, dharmic, lasting injury
Inflicted by a sullen society.
Indifferent to spiritual law, one unswerving fact:
To punish, twice punishes! Never rectifying the vile, ugly act.

Could we choose to do otherwise?

We choose to pay him back: an eye for an eye, a tooth for a tooth!
His parents' lack of love paired with cruelty
Creates a catastrophe visited on us and their next generation.
Like God, we too have turned away from a truth.
Society could find protection. It could still seek other, kinder, re-creation.

Could we be our best and not do otherwise?

Reflections on
"A Trail of Dried Tears"

Suffering, like joy, is part of all our lives. As we grow from infancy to the years as toddlers, as adolescents, as adults, for many the proportion of suffering overtakes joy. There are many who suffer unfortunate accidents of nature. These accidents are bearable. But for most of us, the suffering that inflicts lasting harm comes from those we love and those who love or should love us. These acts may stem from addiction and neuroticism. They consist of sadism, narcissism, uncontrolled anger, jealousy, fear, or dependency. To the degree that an individual's acts are not predictable, consistent, and reality based, they inflict injury. When these acts are unpredictable and whimsically violent, enduring injury to the capacity to love and trust occurs. For the victim, an unacceptable response to pain and frustration becomes a lifetime habit. There is no defense but withdrawal alternating with rebellion. The effect is that one learns that love wounds, not that love enhances joy, hope, and trust.

It is as if we are plants. Given wholesome genes, good soil, abundant sunlight, and adequate nourishment, plants grow and adapt. Variations must be within bearable limits. If variations exceed the capacity to adapt, the plant dies before reproducing. So it is with children. Loving a child increases their capacity to adapt; without love, vulnerability to the whimsical injurious acts of the parents increases. The boundaries of adaptability are broached. These injuries heal by scarring. These disabled and scarred children cannot either give or receive normal loving. Their injury has deprived them of the nurturing emotions: trust, empathy, sympathy, appreciation, and gratitude. They engender their disability on their children.

Almost all serious criminals who are young and who act impulsively have suffered these types of injuries. In addition, most have suffered perinatal neurological injury and/or genetic predisposition to addiction. They have committed frightful acts of cruelty. The origin of these behaviors is the result of their parenting. The incubation period of this disorder is many years. To be activated, it requires many injurious events throughout a lifetime. This is a failure of morals. It is a failure of kindness, concern, and thoughtful action by our society for these children. Their acts are not willful in nature. Rather they are the result of long-term learning. Society bears considerable responsibility for this outcome.

From the beginning of their tragic lives, these children are destined to commit crimes. And society denies all responsibility for the injury inflicted on them. We do not protect these children from the wounding acts of their loved ones. How can we rationally demand that the perpetrators be responsible ten to thirty years after the damage has been done? To demand that the criminal bear full responsibility decades after the injury that made such acts inevitable borders on the bizarre. Yet that demand, it is commonplace. The well-meaning people of our judicial system, including the trier of fact (the members of the jury or the judge) have not yet faced the real problem. They believe the defendants bear all the responsibility. This attitude is pathetically defensive, self-righteous, and self-serving. It denies established fact. It obliterates any responsibility society might exercise to prevent the crimes. The trier of fact does not see society as culpable even though society allowed such injury to be inflicted for years. If a genie could collapse time and by so doing dramatize the horrific acts against these children, anyone would be compelled to intervene. However, taking into account the private nature of the acts, the long incubation period for abnormal behavior to appear, the inherent difficulty and expense of taking effective preventive action, it is comforting to point out that all people have suffered. Society through the judicial system righteously maintains that many who suffer never act illegally. However, all suffering is not equal nor are sufferings' effects. The reason is that all people who suffer are not biologically the same. While meting out punishment to criminals, the triers of fact and our society wash their hands of any responsibility to the perpetrator. The truth is that it is society's responsibility to remedy these ills when they happen, long before the defendant's offense takes place. Society is the only agent powerful enough to change what is foreordained.

We must turn our backs on planned and rationalized vengeance to a more humane treatment that protects society from the violent and devastating acts of adults who were wounded as children. This proposed policy would have two prerequisites: One, it would require empathy, sympathy, and rationality, but most importantly, the capacity of society to shoulder its fair responsibility for not having acted expeditiously. Two, it would require sizable expenditures and thoughtful planning to provide a humane but restricted environment that both protects society from the heinous acts of these wounded individuals and provides for maximum healing and self-development insofar as that is clinically possible.

Do you realize there are no other populations of our society, disabled to this degree, that are not at least theoretically entitled to our best therapeutic efforts? Our society hides behind the hostile rationalizations of the most primitive tenets of the Old Testament. A common view particularly but not exclusively mounted by conservatives is that this behavioral defect of the mentally ill criminal is simply the result of inherent evilness. Therefore, the well-intentioned lawmakers, the professional participants in the judicial system, and the trier of fact operate on the concept that the criminal deserves cruel and prolonged ostracism rather than civil and humane treatment within a restricted environment. This phenomenon is a primitive, unconsciously derived, and sadistic blot on our civilization. With such a perspective, we need not feel guilt. We need not shoulder any responsibility nor bear any shame for wounds inflicted though out a lifetime. We have passively allowed this to happen during the upbringing of these young persons. Through this awareness, we could rise above our base instinct of vindictive punishment to a rational, righteous, humane, and fair policy to deal with criminals within the considerable restraints necessary to protect society from their acts.

Can't We Even Put Our Children in the Garbage Can?

> "The greatness of a nation can be judged by the way its animals
> are treated." This is attributed to Gandhi. I would change it to "The
> way its animals, the insane, and criminals are treated."

What a fastidious nation!
In this, toss all our cans.
In that, only our glass.
In boxes, every scrap of paper.
All in its special place, its station.

From our tidy homes they're taken
To the press for cans,
To the furnace for glass,
Grinders for paper.
Everything sold for just a token.

Recycle all material things
To preserve our resources.
We work and struggle,
Fighting for money, evading trouble,
We plan to dodge need's stings.

What of our loves' bids on eternity?
Our children, treasures born of pain and hope,
Sliding down a path
From a peak at birth
Into enclosing canyons of uncertainty.

Washed with lush placental sustenance,
Nurtured with vitamins and minerals,
Stimulated by hormones born of love,
Aged by a mother's warmth and moisture,
Babes break out with wailing countenance.

They are on a certain descent from conception's peaks.
They may have been tainted by speed, coke, and gin.
They may have been rocked to love's fine motion.
They may have suffered maternal battery.
From hideaways, they glide out on amniotic leaks.

Their course is molded by parental karma.
Either traumatized by noxious stimuli
Or caressed into a loving, humane life
Or simply supplied with something in between.
Their course is shaped by some detached Buddha.

If that course unleashes societal destruction,
Failing to develop all their humane potential
Or sends them on a lessened life of drug abuse
Or pushes a tortured mind into frenzied killing,
Society treats these defectives with firm resolution!

Unlike our glass,
Unlike our cans,
Unlike our paper,
So carefully recycled,
We seek energy to destroy them.
We find purpose in shunning them.
We spend money to punish them.

They are not worth another arduous cycle.
We refuse to carry them back to the peak of birth
For a different run in a happier, more humane canyon of life.
    That is too forgiving for us!
    That is too soft and kind for us!
    That is too expensive for us!
    That takes too much effort for us!
We do not value their lives so much,
Or our own pecuniary self-interest,
To forgo self-righteous vindictiveness
To shape our criminals with a caring, healing touch!

Reflections on "Can't We Even Put Our Children in the Garbage Can?"

What does a bottle cost us? How much do we save by saving them? I am sure it is a significant amount, considering the millions we use. What about recycling oil? How much do we save? Hours and hours of tedious, sometimes dangerous toil, filled with mind-numbing drudgery. And paper? Stripping the foothills and mountains, scarring them with clear cuts, diminishes the most priceless intangible: the elation from viewing unspoiled nature. Our efforts at recycling stem from fear of want—want for resources that are a prerequisite for a rewarding, fulfilling life. This is an effort deserving support. It benefits not only us but future generations. Let us do it wholeheartedly until our sun dies or a meteor strikes Earth, pulverizing everything.

Where do our children come into this process? We want them to have enough. Almost all parents have sacrificed something of value to provide something of value to their children. It is a satisfying, natural, and reflexive act. Our culture has progressed to the point where some things are not particularly apparent, yet important. Awareness is essential in setting priorities. The most important resource we have is our children. And we squander them. We send them to fight to maintain power of our politicians, and many die. Others are wounded in body, and many more are maimed in spirit. We glorify the terror and dehumanization of warfare. Bravery, camaraderie, and excitement feed those who are hungry for meaning among us, especially among those whom we select or those who are self-selected for cannon fodder.

We set our hopes on our children. How devastating to leave life certain that our children will not live humane lives. Setting aside the moments of mindless passion in conceiving them, once our children are conceived, we want them to achieve happiness, gratification, and meaningful lives. These desires for our children are lifelong motivations. Even those parents who wound do so out of weakness, mental illness, and desperation—that is, unintentionally. What we have done before and what we do after molds their life course. We have fashioned a constrained path for them, the children. That path limits them to a specific range of humanity. After a few years, we could choose to fashion a different course. That choice is costly in energy, will, resources, money, patience, and understanding. It is a monumental task. Yet it would be heartbreaking if we fail to correct our mistakes in parenting.

If our child becomes destructive to society, parents are, at first, offended by the accusations of the authorities, then pained by the truth in the accusations. Society's judicial machinery lays waste to much more than the child. A mindless juggernaut, it crushes relatives and obliterates futures. It is a machine fine-tuned to spread emotional turmoil. It wastes the energy of those who seek to defend as well as those who prosecute. It slams the door on freedom though it achieves an environment that protects society. At the same time, it labels juvenile criminals not worth saving or redeemable. They live forever believing they are not worthy of trust or kindness. Even in the case that a youngster lives a life within the constraints of the law, the message of being an evil miscreant is firmly engrained. Society convinces him that he is evil by using stringent conditions of incarceration.

Most who service the judicial system are well-meaning. They do not begin by communicating this demeaning message to juveniles. The system blunts, then exhausts their will. Our prison system is not a wholesome and life-affirming environment for either caretakers or inmates. It should be our goal to make it so. No matter what we preach, what we do is more convincing.

How much does how we treat our young inmates cost in time, ongoing expenses, and loss of future benefits? How much in intangibles: emotional pain and grief, trashed family ties, community clucking about youth violence? No accountancy can specify the physical, much less emotional, losses. Having labored in this system for twenty-eight years, I testify to the long-term suffering and profligate consumption of resources resulting from just one serious offense, such as murder or rape. It is mind-boggling and immense.

Who can cut our losses? Only voters can. Politicians follow votes, reluctantly when voting constrains their power. Inevitably, slowly they follow votes. What price is our lack of forgiveness? How cheap is effective humane treatment and management by comparison?

Why have we rejected comprehensive rehabilitation of our criminal young, a significant part of our most valuable resource? By comprehensive,

I mean educational, social, and psychological counseling and treatment. We believe it too expensive. Not so, compared to the cost of prosecution and lifelong incarceration, much less execution. Voters believe the methods at hand are ineffective. Not so, even if recidivism is prevented in only one in four, I believe it would be a cost saving.

More importantly, we discount the intangible costs of the debilitating effect of pursuing vindictive punishment. The people who staff the prisons, execute the criminals, prosecute, defend, and judge the defendants are also injured! They cannot help but ignore the pain and suffering of those who bore, loved, or were friends of the innocents and miscreants alike. They are largely indifferent or are unaware of the shattering effect on those few who are falsely proven guilty. What about the saintlike or eminently practical (from my perspective) relatives and loved ones of victims who are repelled by the punishment handed out? And what is the cost to those close to the victims who take pleasure in the punishment? How long does this impact these people after the punishment has been accomplished?

What does the criminal learn from punishment? Admittedly, there are deterrent effects. But there are costs to society from what the average criminal learns. What does he learn from vengeful punishment, degradation of the current prison environment, estrangement and isolation, long-term boredom, lack of forgiveness, and absence of serious efforts toward rehabilitation? After all, even if the efforts of rehabilitation lead to failure, which is not always true, at least the communication inherent in that effort says that the criminal is worth the effort. I am in no position to measure accurately these multiple deleterious effects. But taken together, it is obviously a very steep price to pay for revenge. Rather we should engage in serious rehabilitation with adequate societal safeguards. By adopting rehabilitation and safety rather than safety and revenge, we make a statement about ourselves. That message would be that we value all life and will use all practical means to render all lives valuable.

Not to Forgive, Wasting Life

In 1997, PBS aired a program on the Rwandan genocide entitled "Valentina's Nightmare." It is a documentary detailing the mutilation of Valentina and the extermination of the Tutsi community living in Nyarubuye. This killing field was in a courtyard of a Catholic church, where the victims sought sanctuary but received none. In April of 1994, the killing was performed with great cruelty. This courtyard, containing the mutilated remains of the victims, is now preserved as a memorial to all the victims of the Rwandan genocide, numbering one million. This genocide took place and was in some instances supported and not in any substantial way hindered by the civilized countries of the world. Not only did the first-world countries do nothing, but even African countries did nothing to stop the massacre.

Bodies were strewn akimbo across a churchyard of sorts,
Only part of Valentina's story;
Hiding in the blood of her family's hacked body parts,
Only part of Valentina lives on.
Only a cog in the gears of man's cyclical genocide,
Rwanda is only part of an old story,
A predictable product of those in power who lied.

This chanted stock lie
Leads so many to die.
"There is something less than human"
In those about whom the politician lie.
Will we ever learn to be stone-deaf to mean men?

They mislead, only loosing power makes them cry!

Not first, but hopefully among the last,
Are Rwanda's lost children, the families torn?
Society's competence shredded.
Punishing now and forever, generations set apart.
The fabric of life, misshapen, miswoven, it's base relief—
Indelible, inevitable, durable, an ugly and tragic picture.
We *will* change through learning and the tears of embraced grief.
We *will* make man's future, the path to a state, more humane, artful, richer.

Can we not learn from this cruel, ever-present history?
What could we do to weave, shape a soaring, seamless story?
We will achieve a world fashioned by us, leading
"Leaders" crazed by power in hesitating advance, bringing
Fruition to imagined affection and kindness toward all
Who embrace others as separate, yet one, as life's wards.
It is not a choice—it is inevitable—just as water flows to its lowest level.
It is hard, though simple: man, woman, child, arm in arm, move to ever
higher level.
Note that men and women, armed, march in uniformity in rank and file,
Loving, they laugh, saunter arm in arm, each along a branched enthralling trail?

Choosing not to know, we turn our faces away from
So many Rwandas: Cambodia, Vietnam, the Holocaust.
By doing so, you and I are coconspirators in these crimes
Instigated by power-obsessed politicians. We stave off that inevitable time
When life is held precious,
When difference is honored,
When all by loving all of life
Are loved, rather than trapped, by self.

"In remembrance is the secret of redemption."
We will see squarely
That liars lusting for power turn loved ones into bleached bones,
Machete, gas chamber, imprisonment, torture—
Acts of arrogant indifference.

But we renounce vengeance.
We will bring those liars to a just and blind bar.
We will not deform justice
To satisfy bloodlust springing from grief and loss.
Not that they do not deserve to bear that terrible cross;
We will not live with the knowledge that we bent justice
Hypocritically, quenching flames set by their sadistic, grasping vice.

Justice must be used by us to set love's course—certain and straight.
To ease our spirits, souls, bodies from pain initiating new pain,
Through a humane alchemy, we choose the enhancing liberty of fairness,
Bringing to political liars justice's corrective and long-memoried might.

Complimentary Poem to
"Not to Forgive, Wasting Life": Standing By

If I am not concerned for myself, who will be?
But if I am only concerned for myself, what good am I?
And if now is not the time to act, when will it be?

—Hillel the Elder

What is self-interest?
Can you watch pain without feeling?
Can you see injury without suffering?
Where does thinking come in?
Balancing these questions, I claim:
From fantasies, our feelings spawn our acts.
Thought intrudes between our fantasies and our acts,
Preordaining inaccurate future facts.

Outrage purchased cheap,
An indulgence in rectitude,
Absent self-knowledge is costly, thoughtless.
What is the real per-unit cost of responding out of outrage?
It creates despair much too dear to bare.

And we nurture our self-serving immortal lies.
"I did not know."
"I was busy."
"Others do it too."
"I don't believe it."

"I did not see it."
"I misunderstood."
"Others should fix it."
"They did not see it."
"I think charity starts at home."
"Why just me? I am the good guy."

We cherish convenient ways of shifting responsibility,
Bypassing, dodging out of harm's way.
So we fail to act and are surprised when it happens to us.
If we were certain that we would pay,
Could we sanctify ourselves but endanger our lives and act?

But we could do something even if it does not work!
We could give something of ourselves.
What are your parameters of altruism?
How far from your skin does altruism flow?
Do not answer quickly! Think.
The answer will make us cringe.

To which our self-interest sticks.
Outside, lives our indifference and feigned ignorance.

Fantasy inspired by modern communication:
Cruelty comes into our living rooms,
A serious sauce for our frozen TV dinners,
Making us thankful for antacids,
More often than not bringing a taste of bile.
We are sure, though we dare not admit it.

Stare at ourselves, walking cold, exhausted, shattered.
        Are you different than those who
        Kill, rape, torture, displace, abuse?
        Will you just look bravely inside?
        Can you own it, others so to use?

Be careful when speaking of ghastly acts.
For we all treasure that self-same cruelty.
The first step for elevating altruism to the fore
Is not to follow blindly our innate and human
Capacity to kill, rape, torture, displace, abuse.
Not to give in to what would relieve love-forged pain.
Altruism shields process from base purpose.

Do no harm! Always, on your will, act!
An analogue to the physician's Hippocratic oath,
"Do no harm," for all of us, the primary dictum.
The second empowering dictum: Act!

We can never be fully certain that we are right—
That we have understood all ramifications.
We can never be sure that our cause is just—
Is the worthy goal a just altruism?
You must befriend what poisons our process
To admit what excites sensual and bloody lust.
Fear relief in vindictiveness, which mangles souls!

Cadaverous faces on those who drag the dead to unearned graves,
The spectral horror of slaughtered dead
To graves scooped by tractors' blades.
If we look inside, we see ourselves dragging those dead,
Dragging, dragging . . .

Reflections on "Not to Forgive, Wasting Life" and "Standing By"

> *Justice requires power, insight, and will* and *He who does not punish evils commends it be done.*
> —Leonardo Da Vinci as quoted in *How to Think Like Da Vinci* by Michael J. Gelb

Perhaps I've overlooked something, but I contend that forgiveness is a prerequisite to cultural advancement. It is essential to personal, ethical, psychological, and cultural progress. It is a product of right living for everyone. It is left to religious disputes. It is practically absent in discussions of law and peace.

There is a Holocaust memorial by Eric Segal in Golden Gate Park in San Francisco. The inscription reads, "In remembrance is the secret of redemption." It would seem remembrance is the first step in achieving forgiveness, but it is not sufficient.

Redeem is defined, "To buy back, to get or win back, to be free from distress or harm, to extricate from or help to overcome something detrimental, to release from blame or debt, to be free from the consequences of sin, to change for the better, to restore, to convert into something of value, to offset a bad effect." When we think of war crimes and genocide, the concept of redemption must be applied to those who suffer and to those who caused suffering. This applies to those who stand by without doing anything—from the lowliest, slavish perpetuator to the person in power who has, by evil manipulation, promoted acts of genocide. For an act to be redeemed, the memory must be vivid and enduring. To enable forgiveness, remembrance must be devoid of disabling emotion. Who can experience joie de vivre while feeling the impact of senseless, willful, and cruel destruction of the innocent or even of the guilty?

Keeping tragic experiences alive is my daily professional fare. They are the essential core of psychotherapy, whether tragedy be dealt with through tears or laughter. Bad things happen. Even so, we cannot allow ourselves to be overwhelmed and destroyed by them. We must accept and then incorporate the experience into our whole being, even to the point of its being a part of one's day-to-day life—that is, feelings, thoughts, and behavior. To achieve this, emotion associated with the injuries must be diminished so that the acts themselves may neither be forgotten nor denied. This is accomplished with understanding and tolerance—that is, through forgiveness. Sometimes, the mechanism is therapeutic desensitization, sometimes tincture of time or religious faith. An injury must never be condoned, supported, or in any way accepted. The feelings of the victims and their families—grief, loss, and despair—must be integrated into their personalities. While feelings of the perpetrators—anger, righteousness, and self-satisfaction—must be understood and worked through by themselves, leading to an insightful state where the rights and lives of victims are respected and honored. Vengeance by survivors and their families, as opposed to just retribution, must be set aside. It is nothing less than the pathological and self-damaging outcome of tragic experiences. Not doing so makes repetition of genocide a certainty. Ultimately, the normal follow-up of remembrance is forgiveness. Forgiveness protects us from the repetition of genocide without crippling our will through grief and despair. Forgiveness does not diminish our humanity through the survivors' and their families' judicial or social manipulation of the perpetrators.

Failures to forgive are as devastating to the victims as they are poisonous to permanent prevention. The failure to forgive creates bitterness and vindictiveness. It makes us willing to work around normal ethical considerations to gain revenge. If ethical retribution cannot be visited on those responsible, one pattern of this failure is self-loathing. A common devastating outcome is draconian punishment on those who bear minor or subordinate roles in genocides. True, they must be held to account. But it is more important and more effective that those who were in power be brought to justice swiftly, publicly, and fairly. Every detail of the misery they caused should be meticulously documented and widely publicized. Doing so provides the survivors and their family with comfort and hope for the future. It not only provides a rational path to the future; it provides a warning to those who abuse their power. It convinces the survivors and their relatives that what they have accomplished by just retribution is a service to all future generations. It honors the victims. Just retribution must be apportioned according to the degree of voluntary engagement in the acts of genocide. If we follow these guidelines, we can be proud of retribution and confident in effectiveness in preventing recurrences. Without justice, tolerance, understanding, and forgiveness, redress has no value. By doing so, we enhance the ethical and spiritual evolution of cultures, societies, and mankind. Justice nurtures what we need most. It expands wisdom and strengthens our resolve. It prepares us for a future free of war, crimes, and genocides.

While accurate, fair, pervasive, balanced, and unbiased remembrance of events is a prerequisite to redemption, another essential ingredient to political, social, and psychological communal and individual health is even-handed justice. Justice, carried out with the rights of the wrongdoers properly and ethically protected, not only serves to protect the injured from a repetition of genocide but also serves as a warning to those that follow that they too will be held responsible for their behavior. Application of justice must be ordered in some sort of rational priority. It serves to provide those wronged with hope for the future and some modicum of comfort in their remembrance of the pain inflicted on them and their loved ones. It shows the survivors a path to the future, bypassing the awful and profoundly degrading feelings associated with vindictiveness and revenge outside of appropriate and measured justice. It promotes in the survivors the secure knowledge that what they have done to achieve redemption is just, moral, fair, and most importantly, a service to the future of their descendants. It honors the victims. It should be prioritized according to the level of volition exercised by perpetrators. If so, we can be proud of our acts of holding perpetrators responsible for their actions. Without justice as well as tolerance and understanding, redress is without redeeming value for us. With justice, it services and promotes the ethical and spiritual evolution of cultures, societies, and mankind in general. It provides what we need most; it enlarges our humane wisdom and strengthens our resolve for a future free of war crimes and genocide.

The Sea's Mirrored Grace

What if I only loved you?
    What? you ask, I *only* love you?
Yet there is this thing between us.
    I move in, tire, trail away.
You receive me, drawing out my curling form,
    Then rest, waiting patiently for my return.
I become you—your sand changes to our sky mirror.
    You become me—my foam brightens your sun-dried sand.
We have been like this for eons.
    So lovers and loners alike
Stroll through our mirrored grace—
    Their fates vanishing like fading footprints.

Reflections on "The Sea's Mirrored Grace"

When I am by the sea, I feel how painful its ever-changing beauty is. The sea has drawn me to her relentlessly all my life. When I am away from her, I yearn for her. My thoughts cannot contain my yearning; it is part of my mind, just as lymph is part of my tissue.

The surf bears no malice; it simply manifests the laws of physics. The surf washes in and out, mauling and caressing the shore. Even so, the crashing or lapping waves and their paint-like washing reorders the shore at every instant, just as the shore reorders the sea. When the sea undercuts a cliff or drives the sand downwind, is it not an intense intimacy between the two? Could this be a model for our love for one another? Love without judgment, without demands, but rather with the simple act of loving and taking by being alive. Within all this lives the pathos of impermanence, at the seashore and in the acts of loving.

LOVE

Love,
Give me the time to persist.
Give me the strength to persevere.
Give me the will to be disciplined and focused.
Give me the intelligence to choose the most efficient path.
Give me the courage to always be humane and kind.
Give me the wit to be happy.
Give me the wisdom to use Love's methods to accomplish Love's aims.

THE END

Edwards Brothers Malloy
Oxnard, CA USA
November 25, 2014